Success!

The Straight-A Guide

A Guidebook
for At-Risk Youth
and Young Offenders

Michael G. Santos

APS Publishing
Encino, CA

Michael Santos gratefully acknowledges the following sponsors who make his work possible:

Academy Press
Axelrod-Zachary
    Family
California Wellness
    Foundation
Fullmer Family
Golden State
    Lumber
Hager Pacific
    Properties
Harbaugh Family
Kathleen Hays
Hendricks and
    Partners
Hercules Medical
    Center

Thomas Hillier, Esq.
Karis Family
Law Offices of
    Jonathan Solovy
Josh Mukai
Nobmann Family
Paperny Family
Sierra Point Lumber
United Pacific
    Forest Products
The Michael G. Santos
    Foundation
The Reyes Family
    Foundation
Ufkes Family

Please consider sponsoring Michael's work. For information on becoming a sponsor contact: Sponsorship@MichaelSantos.org or visit www.MichaelSantos.org

Endorsements

People think that prisons are "country clubs." They are not. People think that prisons deter people from committing crimes. They do not. People think that everyone who goes to prison is getting "just deserts." This is far from true in many, many cases. People think that going to prison means getting a chance at rehabilitation. Maybe, but not likely. Michael Santos has written volumes about prison in America, and his work goes farther than any single body of literature I know to filling in the blank spots in the American consciousness about incarceration. He is by no means a typical prisoner. He is thoughtful, self-critical, and reflective. His enormous energy and potential are squandered in prison time.

Todd R. Clear, Ph.D.
Rutgers University

That Mr. Santos has maintained his humanity, individualism, and indeed his self-esteem in an environment that tends to obliterate these traits speaks volumes to the success of the strategies he has developed. Readers of all ages can learn from Mr. Santos' description of discipline, commitment, and making values-based and goal-centered decisions empowered him to excel and come out of prison whole.

Sam Torres, Ph.D.
California State University, Long Beach

Michael G. Santos is undoubtedly unique within the Federal Bureau of Prisons. Not only is he serving an unheard of lengthy sentence for a non-violent crime, but during his more than twenty four years of incarceration he has been awarded bachelor's and master's university degrees, published several books, contributed articles to scholarly journals, encyclopedias, and edited volumes, and participated in programs to encourage other prisoners to take steps to earn their freedom.

George F. Cole, Ph.D.
University of Connecticut

Success!

The Straight-A Guide

A Guidebook for At-Risk Youth and Young Offenders

Michael G. Santos

APS Publishing
PO Box 260461
Encino, California 91426

ISBN-10 0983134014 / ISBN-13 9780983134015

For information visit www.MichaelSantos.org.

Forward

Joan Petersilia
Adelbert H. Sweet Professor of Law
Stanford University

As someone who has studied the prison system for more than 30 years, I find myself at a total loss for words when I get phone calls from convicts, parents, or family members asking questions like:

* How do I prepare for going to prison?

* What will my day be like in prison?

* How can I help my son or daughter adjust to prison and prepare for release?

* Will my son or daughter ever be able to get a job after prison?

I now have the perfect answer for all of those questions: just read Michael Santos's books! He has done a great service for us all.

Michael writes beautifully and intelligently about some of the most complex issues of our time. He writes about the lifelong implications that accompany poor decisions he made as a young man and he tries to persuade others to think beyond the thrill of the immediate moment.

I highly recommend Michael Santos's books to juvenile justice personnel, teachers, and families who struggle to help young people understand reasons why they should think about the consequences that frequently follow transgressions.

If we listen to him closely, we may well understand why America's experiment with mass incarceration has failed. That would not only be good for Michael, who will be released from prison soon, but for the rest of society who thinks "what goes on in prisons, stays in prisons." Rather Mr. Santos teaches us that "what goes on in prisons eventually comes back to communities." We should all pay heed to his experience and recommendations for system change. I highly recommend this book to anyone interested in prison reform and community justice.

Joan Petersilia, Ph.D.
Stanford Law School

To my loving mother and grandmother,
and the memory of
my father and grandfather,

I apologize for the
heartache my bad decisions
have caused.

Other Books by
Michael G. Santos

Inside: Life Behind Bars in America
(St. Martin's Press)

About Prison
(Wadsworth/Thompson Press)

Profiles From Prison
(Greenwood/Praeger Publishing)

Prison! My 8,344th Day
(APS Publishing)

Earning Freedom
My Triumph Over a 45-Year Prison Term
(APS Publishing)

For more information visit
www.MichaelSantos.net

The will to succeed is important,
but what's even more important
is the will to prepare.

Bobby Knight
College Basketball Coach

Contents

Preface

Every day, millions of people in their teens and early 20s make decisions without considering where such choices will lead. Despite the wisdom that parents, teachers, and counselors provide, some find it difficult to make the connection between today's choices and actions with tomorrow's successes and failures. I learned such lessons the hard way.

In 1982 I graduated from high school with mediocre grades. Despite my diploma, I didn't have a clear direction and the temptations of a fast life easily influenced me. Choices I made led to problems with the criminal justice system, and five years after high school a federal judge slammed me with a 45-year sentence.

I've been locked in prisons of various security levels since 1987, when I was 23. During that time I've learned a strategy that has enabled me to grow and lead a meaningful life. Had I understood that strategy during my reckless transition between adolescence and adulthood, I would have made better decisions, avoiding problems with the criminal justice system altogether.

As the months of imprisonment turned into years, and the years turned into decades, my commitment to emerge from prison successfully grew. I could see the pattern more clearly. Without direction, I would always live as a prisoner, susceptible to influences around me. But if I lived with deliberate purpose, watching every step and embracing a total commitment to conquering the difficulties around me, I could lead a life of relevance. Anyone could do it. All that was necessary was a commitment to what I have come to call The Straight-A Guide.

The Straight-A Guide isn't a secret or strategy that any particular individual who is alive today can take credit for having discovered. Leaders have relied upon the strategy since the dawn of mankind. They may not have called it by the same name, but those who reached significant goals made the same types of values-based decisions described in the Straight-A Guide.

Those of us who rely upon the Straight-A Guide to succeed use it as a compass. It leads us out of the vicious cycle of failure that ruins so many lives. We begin with positive *attitudes*. We cling to *aspirations* with clear visions of success, as we define it. Then we take deliberate and decisive *actions*. We hold ourselves *accountable*, and we encourage others to do the same. We create an *awareness* to hone in on opportunities. That awareness leads to incremental *achievements*, and we celebrate them all. Finally, we express *appreciation* for the blessings that come our way.

In the pages that follow, three other prisoners and I describe our efforts to introduce these concepts to a group of at-risk adolescents and young offenders. The outreach program in which we participate represents a part of our commitment to reconcile with society for the bad decisions we made as younger men.

Michael G. Santos
January, 2011

Chapter One

First Impressions

Early on a sunny morning, our counselor from the Federal Prison Camp drives Julius Lige, Kenny Lumpkin, Osvaldo Gonzalez, and me to a local high school. It isn't a regular school where young men and women think about Friday night football games and the pizza parties that follow.

When we turn into the parking lot we see fences covered with coils of razor wire around the school. We walk through gates with electronically controlled locks. We walk through metal detectors like those in airports or higher-security prisons. Many of the students, all young men, look hard rather than cheerful, and they are older than those in a normal high school.

The other three prisoners and I follow our counselor, Ms. Martin, into the large classroom. She walks to the back of the room to sit behind the students and we take the chairs that have been set out for us in the front, beside the blackboard. Students watch us, evaluate us. In a corner we see a man chewing gum as he watches over every movement. On his side he wears a leather holster and the pistol he packs looks threatening. He's a representative of the criminal justice system and he's on post, ready to keep order. But he's not there to watch us. The guy with the gun is there to watch the students.

Kenny Lumpkin is the only one of us who doesn't sit. He has black hair, an olive complexion, and the stance of a middle-aged man whose hardened presence comes with years of exercise in prison. As the senior member of our outreach group, he introduces us, telling the 42 students who sit before us that our counselor has brought us from the prison to share our stories.

"You're going to hear from each of us," Kenny tells the students who look at him with blank faces. "We'll be open to any questions you have about our backgrounds, our imprisonment, and our expectations of what we're going to face when we finish our sentences. I'll give you my story a little later. Our first speaker today is going to talk about his background, but his real message describes a strategy that helps us all. It's one that we think you should consider embracing."

Kenny looks over at me, nods, and we exchange places. The students sit staring, lukewarm in their welcome.

"My name is Michael G. Santos," I begin, wanting their attention. "I've been a federal prisoner since August 11, 1987, and I've served many years in prisons of every security level. I'm serving a 45-year sentence because I began making stupid decisions when I was about your age. Instead of continuing on to college or trade school after high school, I joined friends in a scheme to sell cocaine. The flash and easy money from selling drugs blinded me from seeing the consequences of my actions."

Then I describe how my thoughts began to change when jailers first slammed the steel gates behind me. Back then, in a jail cell I had more time to think. I spent most of that time with elbows on my knees and my forehead in my hands, sweating anxiety. The noise of the streets didn't distract me. While in a jail cell my thoughts weren't distracted by the various ways I could blow the money that came from the cocaine I sold. Instead, I was stressing over the decades I was about to serve and regretting the decisions that led me to prison.

The young men in the classroom are not strangers to prison. When I ask how many have family members serving time, many of the students raise their hands.

"My dad's serving life at Victorville."

"My brother's locked down in Pelican Bay."

"I got one brother up in Lancaster, another at Lompoc, and my pops is in Atwater." The students become more animated with the talk of prison and some blurt out questions.

"Who you run with?"

"Have you ever stabbed anyone or been stabbed?"

"Did you ever see anyone get killed?"

"Raise your hands and wait for the man to call on you before speaking!" The man with the gun shouts, just like a drill sergeant.

I ignore his outburst. They are asking common questions, but I'm not standing in this classroom to talk about gangs, or stabbings, or murder. I remind the young men that what they see on prison reality shows answers those questions. "I've spent my entire adult life in prison," I tell them. "I've walked through puddles of blood, and I still live with all the pains and pressures of imprisonment. But today I'm here to talk about how I could have made better decisions at 16, 17, 18, and 19. If I would have," I tell the group, "I wouldn't have sold cocaine at 20 and 21. By making better decisions I wouldn't have put myself in a situation where a judge would slam me with a 45-year sentence."

"A homie," one of the young men shoots his hand up. He's wearing a plaid flannel shirt buttoned to the top and a bandage patch on his neck covers part of a tattoo. His head is shaved. Despite the young man's presence in a high school classroom, he looks older, and his eyes belie hostility and suspicion for anything I have to say. He's been around, seen too much. "If you're serving 45 years, why they let you out to come talk with us? My pops is only serving a 10 piece and they won't let him off the yard."

"I'm sorry to hear about your dad, and obviously I don't know his struggle. There was a time when I, too, was locked inside the 40-foot walls of a high-security U.S. penitentiary. I spent the first seven Christmases of my term inside USP Atlanta. But I made decisions that kept me out of trouble, and I want to talk with you about the lessons I learned. They helped me grow. Because of my adjustment decisions, my life is different from what society expects for a long-term prisoner. Administrators lowered my security level. For the next ten years they transferred me to various medium- and then low- security prisons. In 2003 they transferred me to minimum-security-camps. I'm still a prisoner, but my custody level sometimes allows me to come into the community under staff supervision."

"So you been locked down for how long?" he asks.

I can tell he's interested but still not committed to listening to me or trusting what I'm saying.

"I'm in my 24th year."

"You been locked down for 24 years straight?" another young man asks skeptically.

"Hey!" The man with the pistol takes a step forward. "Raise your hand before speaking."

"No, I've completed 23 years; now I'm in my 24th year." I break down the total of my years in prison for the student.

"So what you got left homie?" The young man in the plaid shirt now looks more receptive.

"If I continue to receive all my good time, and the parole board makes a favorable decision, release could come for me within three more years."

The young man grimaces, but nods. He'll hear me out.

"May I ask you a question?"

I want to engage this student because I sense his leadership within the group.

He shrugs his shoulders.

"What's your name?"

"The homies call me Smoke."

"How old are you?"

"I'm going to turn 21 in a couple of months."

"Can I ask if you're here because you want to be here, or do you have to be here?"

"It's part of my sentence, my being here. I'm on probation until I turn 21."

"So in a few months," I inquire, "when you turn 21, you won't have to come anymore?"

"That's right. I'll be a free man."

"Does that mean you won't graduate, or will you earn a diploma?"

"I ain't thinking about graduation right now, homie. All I'm trying to do is finish up this paper."

"Smoke," I walk a little closer toward him, trying to connect with him, "I'm sure the people who run this school invite community leaders here to talk about the importance of education, jobs, and things like that. Each of us," I gesture to the prisoners sitting beside me, "are a little different. We're standing before you as living examples of what happens to people who make decisions without thinking about the future. Now I'm not saying it's a fact that if you don't think about your future you're going to prison. But it is a fact that I didn't think about the future when I was your age. And it is a fact that I've been in prison since before you were born."

"Prison ain't nothin' to me. I been locked up before. I ain't scared."

"I don't doubt that for a minute, and I know you could handle it. I'm not here to scare you with stories about how tough prison is. You could make it. Sure. But wouldn't you like something better for your life? I know I would."

"What I'd like and what's waiting for me might be two different things." He slouches in his chair. I sense the other students identifying with Smoke's hopelessness.

"Have you ever heard of Henry Ford?" I ask.

"Have you ever heard of Ernesto Castillo?" he snaps back, defying me.

"I haven't." I scratch my head. "Should I know him?"

"He's my uncle, doing life without parole, calling shots on the big yard."

"That's what I'm here to talk to you about," I say to Smoke. "Not about serving life in prison, but about how decisions we make can lead to more fulfilling lives—wherever we are, and regardless of what circumstances we're in."

"So why'd you ask me if I knew Henry Ford? Everyone knows Henry Ford."

"Because one of the things Henry Ford is famous for having said strikes me as being accurate. It's something I'd like to share with you."

A young man on the other side of the room, in the front row, only a few steps away from where I stand, raises his hand. On the inside of his forearm I see welts. I recognize them because I've seen them on hundreds of young prisoners. He's been slicing horizontal lines into his arm with a razor—the cuts bleed, then heal badly. "Hold up," he says. "Who's Harry Ford?"

"It's *Henry* Ford, Lump. Not Harry Ford," Smoke corrects him with a sneer.

"So what did he say?"

"Henry Ford was the founder of the company that makes Ford cars and trucks. I'd say that accomplishment distinguishes him as a successful businessman. Wouldn't you?"

Lump nods in agreement. "But what did he say?"

"I'm sure he said many things, but I read somewhere that when he was describing how people think, Mr. Ford said that one kind of man believed he could do anything, and another kind believed he couldn't do anything. Henry Ford said they were both right."

"So," Smoke dismisses the message. "What's the big deal about that? What's that got to do with us?"

"When I heard you say earlier that what was waiting for you might be different from what you want, I wondered which type of person you thought of yourself as. Do you see yourself as the kind of man who can do anything, or do you see yourself as the kind of man who can't?"

"It don't matter how I see myself," Smoke answers me. "I'm representing to the fullest, but I still got to deal with what's up. I got to deal with what's going on in the real world, with people looking at me funny, with no one wanting to give me a job, with probation officers and cops always breathing down my neck, harassing me for nothing. I'm just keeping it real, homie."

"Oh I know you're keeping it real from how you see the world, from the perspective of what you've lived. And I respect that. But we've come here to share a different perspective. We were once your age, dealing with the kinds of pressures that you and everyone else in this classroom have to cope with. We did what we had to do. It wasn't until we were locked in prison with decades to serve that we began to understand that we had options we didn't even know about, options that could have brought different outcomes, better opportunities. That's what we're here to talk about with you." I see a few of the students nodding their heads, receptive to my message.

"So what?" Smoke is still skeptical. "You done did your time and now you want to come out to preach to us about how we're supposed to stay in school, do right, get a job and all that? You think we ain't heard enough of all that, homie?"

"I'm not here to preach anything. All I want to do is to show you some strategies that I wish someone would have shown me when I was your age. You might consider them or you might reject them. That's up to you. They might help you with the certainty that you can do much more than you think possible, regardless of circumstances complicating your life right now."

"Is that all you can do?"

Smoke enjoys challenging me, and I see that he has his followers in class.

"Do you think you can do more, like you want us to do?"

He was mocking me. "You're still locked down after 23 years, right?"

"That's right, I'm in prison. But tell me, Smoke. I can see you're bright, confident, a natural leader. I'm guessing you know about being locked up. How many times have you been in jail?"

"I been going to juvie since I was 13. Been locked up seven, eight times since then."

"I'm sorry to hear that. How about the rest of you? How many of you have been in custody before?"

"They're all on probation," the man with the gun answers for the class. "Some of them leave here and report back to juvenile hall, some go to group homes, some are in foster care. These guys have seen it all."

"Well, if it's true that you've seen it all, then you must have some idea of what it's like to serve a long prison term. Can any of you see yourselves serving 10 or 20 years in prison?"

No hands.

"Maybe you have some idea of how prison shapes a man's life. Tell me what would you expect of a man who surrendered 10 or 20 years, or more to prison? Based on what you've seen in juvenile hall or other prison-type experiences, what do you think would characterize most long-term prisoners' lives?"

"They're angry."

As has been the case, Smoke leads the class in responding.

"Good." I walk to the blackboard and pick up a piece of chalk to write his answers. "Anyone else? If it's okay with the officer, don't bother raising your hands. Just tell me. What does society expect from a person who served a long time in prison?"

The officer nods to give his assent.

"He's bitter."

"He don't have no family ties."

"He can't get a job."

"He's a shot caller on the yard."

"He ain't got no woman in his life."

"He smokes a lot of weed, drinks a lot of pruno."

Some of the students laugh as I bullet point their responses on the blackboard. Then I step back and look at the answers I've written. "So we know what prison is supposed to do to a man, and it doesn't look like a recipe for happiness. And since I've been locked down for so long, those must be the descriptions you would expect for my life." I bring my hand to my chin while considering the descriptions on the board. "Smoke, do I seem angry or bitter to you?"

"Not really. Ain't got no ink on you. You don't even look like you been locked up before."

"You may not realize it, but you pay me a huge compliment when you say that I don't look like I've been locked up before. I've worked very hard to project such an image. And if I succeed in doing so when I'm out, do you know what I expect it to mean?"

"No," he shrugs. "What do you expect it to mean?"

"I expect it to mean that when I join you in the real world, I won't have to worry about people looking at me funny, I won't have to worry about finding a job, and I won't have to worry about probation officers and cops always breathing down my neck, harassing me for nothing. Weren't those the problems you described as having to contend with when you were keeping it real?"

"That's what's up when you live in my barrio, homie."

"I don't know where you live, so maybe you can help me understand. Would you say that your barrio is more or less restrictive than a federal prison?"

"It ain't no prison, homie. I'm not saying that. All I'm saying is it ain't easy going legit with all the pressures out there."

I nod my head in agreement. "I'm with you, Smoke. It's not easy." I walk to the blackboard and I use my finger to reference the bullet points. "It isn't easy making it through a long prison sentence either—especially without becoming angry or bitter—while nurturing family ties, while securing a job to go home to, and while bringing a woman into your life. These are some of the differences that distinguish my prison adjustment from what the prison system, society, and even you guys expected. It's not easy to overcome obstacles, but I've found a strategy that works for me. If the strategy can work to power me through a long prison term and prepare me for my return to society, then I know it can help you overcome the challenges you face."

"What's the strategy?" Smoke asks.

I erase the bullet points of negativity on the blackboard and write Success! The Straight-A Guide.

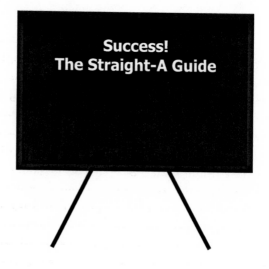

Chapter Two

What's Freedom?

The other men with me sit in chairs beside the blackboard watching my presentation and waiting to share their stories with the students. First, I continue by explaining the Straight-A Guide, hoping that I don't come across as too preachy. The young men in my audience have too many people telling them what to do and giving them orders. It's bad enough that they have to sit in chairs under the watch of a man who packs a pistol, but they also leave school to return to their own mini-prisons. If they embrace the strategy that helps other prisoners and me triumph over the struggles of prison, I'm thinking they might succeed in avoiding it altogether.

After I write the name I gave to the strategy on the board, Smoke pipes in. "So what you did, homie, is discover the secret path to a white house with a white picket fence, 2.2 kids and a new Chevy in the driveway?"

Several students laugh at Smoke's sarcasm.

"Well, is that how you would define success? A house and car?" I'm glad to keep Smoke's attention. If I can engage him, then he can help me show the value of this strategy.

"Not really. That fantasy don't work for me."

"Nor do houses, cars, or material possessions work as a definition of success for me. I'm after something bigger, something more lasting," I explain.

"What are you after, money?"

"When a man lives in prison for as long as I have, Smoke, it feels like living on the moon and watching people's lives in the world from outer space. That perspective has shown me that money isn't a very good indication of success. A person can have money one day and lose it the next, and when people chase money for the sake of money, they frequently end up miserable—in prison cells. Success means something different for me, but we're on the right track when we're trying to define it. That's the first step of the strategy. We have to know what we're after, what we're pursuing. What are you pursuing, Smoke?"

"I ain't pursuing nothing," he shrugs. "I'm just trying to blow through these next couple months and finish up my paper."

"Your time on probation is going to end when you turn 21," I point out the obvious. "That's a certainty you can count on, like the sunrise. When it's time it's time. Do you have any plans for your life?"

"You know how these people are, homie. I been trying to come off paper or supervision of some kind since I was 13. Anything can happen. I can't tell what they're going to come up with next. When I finish probation I'll be done with this class, and I'll see what's up after that, probably try to find a job or something."

"How about someone else?" I ask, addressing the class. "Can any of you tell me about something you're pursuing?"

"I want to get me a 'Benz with some big rims on it."

"Okay. That's a start." I write the response on the board. "Anyone else?"

"I want an iPad."

"How about some bling bling, know what I'm sayin'?"

"I'm looking to come up, dawg, to let the money pile up." The young man offering this bumps fists with the student sitting in the chair to his left while I write his answer on the board.

"I hear that," his friend responds.

"These objects you guys want to pursue," I ask, "do they bring happiness?"

"Heck yeah they make a person happy," the student that Smoke refers to as Lump offers.

"Really? Does a Mercedes, a computer, some jewelry, money make someone happy?"

"They would make *me* happy," Lump insists.

"What would happen if you wrecked your Mercedes, your computer broke down, someone stole your jewelry, or you lost your money? What then? Those difficulties happen to people every day."

"Then I wouldn't be happy." The class laughs at Lump's response.

"So the things on the board make a person happy when he has them, but if he loses them then he loses his happiness too. That's why material objects don't strike me as being very good examples of success. A person can have them one day, but lose them the next. I'm wondering whether you guys can help me find a definition of success that lasts a lifetime, that is worth pursuing, that no one can take away, and that doesn't depend on outside forces."

"You're the one who discovered this so-called secret to success," Smoke takes the lead. "Why don't you tell us?"

"It's not a secret, and I can't take credit for discovering anything. I didn't. What I can do is share with you what I've learned from others, from 'masters'. By paying attention to people whom I consider successful, I've accepted that success can only come from within. No one can give it to you and no one can take it away. It can only be earned or forfeited. Success isn't a secret, but a way of living, a step-by-step journey, and if a person commits to the path, it doesn't matter whether he's in a high-security penitentiary or a barrio filled with despair. Through choices he makes, he can create success that lasts a lifetime, that no one can take away. Success is a state of mind, and it only comes when everything you think, everything you say, and everything you do stays in harmony."

"That's far out."

Smoke makes the sound and gesture as if he's taking a long toke on a joint. "You sound like you been listening to too much Cheech and Chong. What kind of bud you been smoking in there, homie?"

The class laughs.

"Oh, you disagree?" I glance over at Smoke.

"A definition like that can't pay no bills, homie. Are you telling us that you're successful?"

"I'm successful because the circumstances of my life don't define me; I'm successful because through the choices I make, I create my own meaning."

"You been down way too long, dawg."

Smoke and his friends laugh. "What kind of meaning you got in your life when you ain't even got no freedom?"

"I have the freedom to choose how I'm going to respond. I can either complain about the length of my sentence or choose to create opportunities despite the restrictions. I choose the latter and dignity comes because of the choice. I'm the captain of this ship, navigating my way through the storms and high seas of a prison term. From my perspective, that's more freedom than those who perceive outside-forces as determining what happens in their lives. The obstacles they perceive—whether rooted in racism, poverty, obesity, whatever—become their own prison. That kind of prison, one made of excuses, has no release date. The only way to break free from it is to change from within. I found the way to break free, and as a consequence I'm living as that guy Henry Ford said could do anything despite obstacles."

Despite my enthusiasm, I haven't yet erased the cloud of defeatism that hangs in the classroom. Perhaps some of the other prisoners here with me will be more effective. The 42 young men who sit at desks in a grid of six rows and seven columns have all been labeled "at-risk," but in many ways they're prisoners already. They're used to being singled out and told "you've got nothing coming." Before we leave today, I'm hoping that our group can plant a seed of hope, showing them that despite the current circumstances, better choices can create opportunities for better lives.

"What have you been able to do from prison that is so meaningful?" Smoke is still leery.

"Well, earlier you all described what you expected to see in a long-term prisoner. But I can assure you that I'm not angry, bitter, or ill-prepared to return to society. By adhering to the Straight-A Guide that I want to introduce to you, I've opened more opportunities than society expects prisoners to enjoy. Every one of those opportunities brings meaning to my life."

"Like what though?" Smoke pushes.

"I've educated myself, earning a bachelor's degree and a master's degree. Then,

by using what I learned, I created more opportunities that enabled me to generate an income with nothing more than a Bic pen, blank paper, and my mind. My work has introduced me to thousands and helped me build a support network that includes hundreds of community leaders who I didn't know before I started serving my sentence. Most importantly, I have meaning in my life because neither the prison system nor any outside force interferes with my success. Regardless of how long I serve, where I am, or what I have, as long as I commit to the Straight-A Guide, I have a compass that will guide me to meaning in my life."

"Hold up. You're saying you made money while you were locked up. What do you mean? Did you have a hustle? Did you run the poker table, move contraband? Is that how you earned a few cartons of cigarettes? What are we talking about? No one makes any real money from prison except by hustling," insists Smoke who has clear ideas about prison life.

"I don't hustle anything. It was hustling that brought me to prison and I'll never do that again. Everything I do is open, completely transparent, and anyone can do the same as I've done. All it takes is commitment, discipline, and work. The payoff is much more than a few cartons of cigarettes, and instead of bringing more problems from hustling or scheming, the work I do opens up more opportunities."

"How much?" interrupts Lump. "What kind of money can you make from prison? Everyone I know who's locked up asks family to send money in."

With a discussion of money—something tangible—I have the class's attention and I want to hold it.

"We all choose our own path," I point out. "When a man lets circumstances like prison or anything else define him, then he submits to the limits those circumstances impose. If he is going to chart his own course, on the other hand, he begins by studying the circumstances. He learns everything there is to learn about them. Then he makes decisions on how best to proceed. I've read that someone defined insanity as doing the same things over and over and expecting a different result. If I were to make the same kinds of decisions that people expect from long-term prisoners, I would not only be crazy, but I'd be angry and bitter and set on a course for continuing failure. Instead, I make decisions as if I'm charting my own course. That's why my life is different from what society expects of a long-term prisoner."

"What does that mean, to chart your own course?" Smoke asks. "And you haven't answered our question of how you make money from prison."

"For me it isn't about making money, Smoke. Everything I do is about leading a meaningful life, about being relevant—having some significance in the world. I strive to live as something more than a prisoner, to make contributions to society despite the boundaries that restrict me. By focusing on what I can do to become more than a prisoner, and preparing myself in ways to ensure that I never have problems with the law again, I can more effectively evaluate my strengths and weaknesses. With that clarity of thought, I make decisions."

I walk to the blackboard and write "strengths" on one side, "weaknesses" on the other.

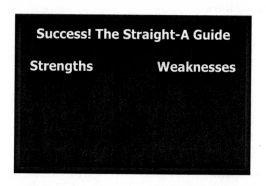

"As crazy as it may sound, I have always seen a potential strength in the length of my sentence. Why? Because if I can master the time instead of allowing the decades I serve to define me, when I conclude my sentence I will have credibility with others, and I can use that credibility to teach. We all encounter adversity in life. Mine happens to be imprisonment. If I can triumph over it, then I become more effective in helping others triumph over their own adversity. From that perspective, I embrace the opportunities that came with lengthy imprisonment because I consider them a potential for strength."

In the column on the blackboard under "strength" I write "long prison sentence." Beneath the column of "weakness" I write "restrictions."

Success! The Straight-A Guide	
Strengths	Weaknesses
Long Prison Sentence	Restrictions

"Prison isn't a cakewalk, as you all know. It comes with obstacles and difficulties. It is my responsibility to understand all of the potential threats. They come from all sides. But by understanding them, I can put myself in a better position to reach the goals I set regardless of the restrictions. Evaluating my own strengths and weaknesses is always one of the first steps I take in charting my own course, and you can do the same."

[47]

"I guess he's not going to tell us how he makes money in prison."

Smoke addresses his classmates instead of me, stirring the ire of the guard who has been sitting on a stool in the corner behind me.

"Show some respect!" the guard orders. "These people come out here to teach you knuckleheads."

The students see my eyes roll. I'm hoping Smoke and his classmates don't associate the other prisoners and me with the guy packing the pistol. The students' respect will only come when they identify with us and the message we present; respect won't come from barked orders or commands.

"I'm an open book, Smoke, and I'll share anything about my life that you want to know. But I don't want to leave you with the mistaken impression that it's the pursuit of money that's driving me. If I were only pursuing money, my life wouldn't be any different from the day I walked into prison. Remember, success for me is a journey, and the destination I pursue is to become a better person, more capable of making positive contributions to the world. By considering how I could contribute from prison, as well as understanding my strengths and weaknesses, I came to the conclusion that I should develop writing skills. I worked every day to become a better writer. By improving my writing skills I improved my thinking skills. And by improving my thinking skills I figured out ways that writing could generate revenues. Then I pursued them."

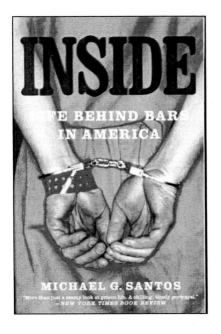

"What do you write, crime stories?" Lump asks.

"I write about the prison experience, mine and others."

"Why do you write about that?"

The young man sitting behind Lump joins the discussion for the first time. He's wearing a bandana around his neck, and I'm guessing he doesn't want to wear it but does in order to comply with school rules about covering up gang-related tattoos.

"I'll tell you," I say to the student with the bandana, "but may I first ask your name?"

"I go by Trey."

"Okay, Trey. Do you know much about prison?"

"Been locked up three times. Guess I know enough that I don't want to go back."

I shake my head. I hate hearing how many young people serve time in cages. "What if you hadn't been? Would you know anything about prison?" I ask.

Trey shrugs his shoulders. "My dad's doing life. I been up to see him a few times, heard what's up from him."

"Prison's tough on families," I say. "I'm convinced that it's much harder on the people who love us. I write about prisons for several reasons. One is that I've spent half of my entire life as a prisoner. Another is that I believe I have a responsibility to share what I've learned as a prisoner with others in order to bring improvements to our nation's prison system. I also write about the prison experience because I want to inspire more prisoners to adjust in ways that will prepare them for better lives upon release and make their lives in prison more fulfilling."

"Hold up, homie," Smoke interrupts. "Do people pay you for writing that?"

"No one pays me anything. Federal prison rules don't allow me to receive payment for my work."

"But you said you was making money in prison," Lump jumps back in.

"That's not what I said."

"Well what did you say?" Lump persists.

"I said my writing generates an income."

"Who gets the income?"

"Many people receive an income from my work. The books I write create income for publishers and those who work for publishers; for the bookstore owners and those who work for bookstores; to the literary agent who represents my work; and for the people in the various businesses that play a role in marketing the books I write. Despite being a prisoner, through writing I'm able to contribute to society, to play a role in it—and because of that it adds value to my life."

"How much money has your writing brought in for people?"

"Several hundred thousand dollars over the years. It's not so much by the standards of the real world, but to have done so from prison—with nothing more than a Bic pen and blank paper—gives me confidence that more opportunities will open when I'm free."

"That doesn't make any sense," Smoke interjects. "Letting other people make all the money from the books you write. Why not sell the books when you get out if the prison won't let you keep the money?"

"Because although prison rules don't allow *me* to earn money from any of my writing, those rules can't interfere with my wife earning money. My work supports her, and that strengthens me."

"How do you still have a wife after all the time you've been locked up?"

"I have a magnificent wife, and although I'm still in prison, we nurture our marriage every day. I told you, my life is different from

what society expects for long-term prisoners and it's not by accident. My life is different because of the choices I make. That's what I want to show you—how to make choices that will open opportunities to improve your life."

"How can you show me, or any of us, how to make better choices when you and your homies are goin' back to the prison at the end of the day?"

For the first time, I sense that Smoke wants to learn. "We'll never see you guys again."

I step back to the blackboard and double underline the words I wrote earlier. "I'm going to show you what we use to succeed. You can use it as your own strategy to achieve what you want. Simply consult the Straight-A Guide."

"What's up with that?"

It's obvious that Trey wants an answer.

Chapter Three

The Straight-A Guide

"The Straight-A Guide isn't a secret recipe and it isn't anything that I've developed," I explain to the students. "When I was in my early 20s, locked in jail for the first time and facing a sentence of life without parole, I understood that bad decisions I had made put me in the predicament I was in. I didn't have any excuses or anyone to blame for the problems my own decisions created. Nor did I know what was going to happen or how long I would really have to serve, but I knew that if I wanted a better life I would have to make changes."

I slowly pace through the grid of desks while I talk.

"That realization led me to begin reading about people who faced struggle in their lives, about people who overcame obstacles—people who faced problems and difficulties with courage instead of excuses triumphed. I learned from those people who lived with a deliberate purpose. They knew what they were after. They made personal sacrifices and commitments to prepare themselves for whatever hardships came their way. I admired their strength and the ways that they contributed to a better world, and I began striving to emulate their leadership. I continue striving today, even after more than 23 years in prison.

"By adjusting to the challenges of imprisonment in the same way those leaders adjusted to their struggles, I empower myself. Whether you're living with restrictions imposed by the criminal justice system or struggling with other difficulties," I assure the group, "you can empower yourselves by consulting The Straight-A Guide for every decision."

While I write and underline each "A" of the guide on the blackboard, I explain that thinking about *Attitude, Aspiration, Action, Accountability, Awareness, Achievement,* and

Appreciation is now automatic for me.

Success! The Straight-A Guide
- ✓ Attitude
- ✓ Aspiration
- ✓ Action
- ✓ Accountability
- ✓ Awareness
- ✓ Achievement
- ✓ Appreciation

"So who were the people you read about? What kind of challenges did they face?" Smoke no longer speaks with the sarcasm that underscored his earlier remarks and I'm pleased to see his interest.

"Have you read about the Holocaust?"

"Wasn't that where the Nazis killed all the Jews?" He's well-read, more than simply street smart.

"That's right. Viktor Frankl wrote about his experiences as a prisoner in the Holocaust. Despite his believing that the Nazis had killed everyone in his family, and his never knowing from one hour to the next whether the Nazis

would kill him, he mustered the strength to embrace every minute of his life. Viktor Frankl's power came from within, from a determination to improve the lives of people around him.

"I also read about Nelson Mandela. Does anyone know who he is?"

"Mandela's president of Africa," Lump answers. "I saw the movie *Invictus*."

"He's president of *South* Africa," I correct him. "But when I read about him I was starting my sentence and he had just been released after serving 27 years. That was about the length of time I expected to serve, and I made a commitment to adjust in ways that would allow me to walk out of prison strong, like Nelson Mandela, regardless of how long I served."

"So is that what you see yourself as?" Smoke asks. "Becoming a politician or world leader when you get out of prison?"

"I'm not comparing myself to either of those great men, Smoke, but they inspire me to become better. No one can overcome all they went through without a strong spirit, without determination, and that is what I strive to build upon every day. I learn from people who fight their way through difficulty. Not only former prisoners, but great athletes like Oscar de la Hoya and people who commit themselves to causes greater than themselves, like Cesar Chavez or Delores Huerta, who fought for the cause of laborers. Those kinds of people don't allow outside influences like the barrio or powerful business forces to deter them from reaching their highest potential. That's what each of you can do if you consult the Straight-A Guide for all of your decisions."

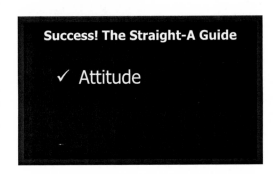

"So what do you mean by 'tude?" Trey asks.

"You're going to see and hear some examples of what I mean by *attitude* soon." I place a check mark beside the word on the blackboard. "Each of the men here with me will share his story, and some will describe how they once hustled on the street and did whatever was necessary to make their stripes. Their attitude was projected by their image as thugs, gangsters, and ballers. The consequence for our choices was a long prison sentence."

Trey raises his hand and then challenges me. "You sayin' that anyone with the 'tude of being a baller is goin' to prison? That's whack. What about Jay-Z, Snoop Dogg, Eminem. They ballers. They ain't locked up."

"Those are performing artists and they project an image to reach a clearly-defined market. I agree with you that each performer you named earns enormous amounts of money because he understands his market, his audience. He's mastered the attitude that helps him sell his music; it's what his fans want to buy. I may be too old for the lingo now, but I think the streets call it "keeping it real."

"That's right," Trey affirms. "They keepin' it real."

"Not completely real, of course. Despite the images of lawlessness those rappers project, they're still abiding by the rules of society in order to reap the benefits of living in society. They're paying tens of millions in taxes to uphold laws that they rap about ignoring; they pay teams of lawyers and advisors for protection. Those rappers aren't keeping it so real that they expose themselves to the criminal justice system. The rappers who do get caught breaking the law will sit in prison, like everyone else."

I engage with several students in the group discussion, trying to explain what I mean by attitude.

"If we turn aside from actors, musicians, athletes, and other celebrities who project attitudes to further their public image, we can more easily understand why The Straight-A Guide begins with attitude. Our attitude reflects how we posture ourselves, how we want others to perceive us. The more we commit to that attitude, the more likely we are to reach the goals we set for ourselves—regardless of what type of attitude or goals we choose.

"I've been standing up here talking for a while now, and what you see in me is what I project wherever I am."

I turn to Smoke.

"How would you perceive me if I came onto your turf?"

"If you came on my turf, one of my homeboys would probably rob you."

The class erupts in laughter at Smoke's response.

"You're probably right. And the reason for that is that the attitude I project—it defines me. Despite the length of time I've served in prison, I don't throw off a vibe that anyone should feel threatened by me."

"You've got that right," Lump says, spawning more laughter.

"If I were trying to project an attitude of being hard, of making an impression on the streets, I'd walk with a swagger. My attitude would show in the way I talked and the way I walked. People from the streets could tell in an instant whether I was real, and they would test me. But if that was the image I wanted to project, I'd have to live with and measure up to all that came with it—I'd be tested. Earlier, Smoke, you described how tough it is in the real world. People look at you suspiciously and law enforcement officers are always harassing you. Do you think the attitude you project might have anything to do with that?"

"No," he answers. "People just judge me by the way I look, discriminate against me right from jump."

"Would you say you project a friendly image of openness, of happiness?"

"I project what I am," Smoke shrugs his shoulders, nonchalantly.

"And in most cases people respond to what they see," I say. "We all carry signs with us and those signs advertise who we are, how we want to be perceived. Those signs include our facial expressions, whether we smile or scowl. They include how we greet each other, even how we walk, how we wear our clothes, groom ourselves, the words and inflection we choose when we talk. The attitude I project may not garner much respect in the 'hood. But I'm not trying to live as king of the streets. I strive to project an attitude that will open opportunities for me and help me reach the goals I set for myself. If I wanted to live as I did before prison, I'd project a different attitude. In doing so, I would have to accept the kind of suspicion and harassment such an attitude invites but that I don't want."

"But a man can't change who he is," Smoke says. "I don't ever want to forget where I came from. I'm representin' to the fullest."

"That's one way of living, Smoke. But it comes with consequences. Since I don't accept that the past defines who I am, I choose another way. I've changed my attitude to become more than what society expects. It's the reason I'm standing here sharing these thoughts with you and your classmates. None of us can choose where we're from, but we can choose where we're going, and our attitudes influence the choices we make. Attitude comes first in the Straight-A Guide because our attitudes determine the level of commitment we make to all else that follows. That leads to the second step.

I place a check mark beside the word "Aspiration" on the blackboard.

Aspiration

Success! The Straight-A Guide

✓ Attitude
✓ Aspiration

"Can anyone tell me what the word *aspiration* means?" I ask the class.

"It's like a wish or something," Lump says.

I consider his response for a second, then elaborate for more clarity. "I suppose that having an aspiration for something is like wishing, but with more substance. We might wish for the impossible, for something we don't have any control over. I wish I never broke the law, for example. But regardless of how hard I wish, there isn't anything I can do to change the past. I wish I hadn't made decisions that

[67]

resulted in my surrendering a quarter century to prison, but that wish won't change anything. I Aspiration to become something more than a prisoner, on the other hand, and because of that aspiration I have more clarity as to what I must do." I walk to the side wall and gesture to the poster of the drill sergeant. "What is the Army trying to imply when it encourages recruits to be all that they can be?" I ask.

"They want people to join and to become soldiers," Trey offers.

"Do you agree, Lump?" His hand is raised and he's nodding his head.

"We're at war. The Army needs soldiers."

"Yes, we need soldiers," I agree, "but the Army is much more than a fighting force. It grooms people for leadership and it offers exceptional training for those who Aspiration to reach their fullest potential. It provides a step-by-step path for those who have the courage and the character and the discipline to commit."

"Sounds like you're recruiting," Smoke says.

"I'm not qualified to recruit, but I'll say this much. Serving in the armed forces would have been much better than serving prison time. The bad decisions I made when I was your age disqualified me from the honor of military service, though I've modeled my adjustment on what I've read about military training. That's how I came to place so much emphasis on the importance of a 100 percent commitment to a positive attitude, and it's the reason I believe that the attitude we choose leads to our aspirations."

I walk to the blackboard and I draw a circle on the left side.

"Okay Smoke," I say while pressing the chalk in the circle on the board, "tell me where to draw."

"What do you mean?" he asks.

"I'm following your guidance. You direct me on what I draw with the chalk."

"How am I supposed to tell you what to draw? I don't know what you want to draw."

"Lump, can you tell me what to draw?"

He shrugs his shoulders, indifferent.

I move to the right side of the blackboard and draw another circle.

"This might help," I say, and walk back to the left side of the blackboard, pressing my chalk into the center of the circle.

"Smoke, if I wanted to connect this circle to the other circle, how would you direct me to draw?"

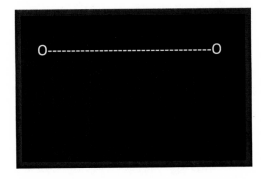

"Just draw a straight line."

"Okay. That's what I'm trying to illustrate," I say while drawing the straight line that connects the two dots. "The shortest route between two points is a straight line. But without a clear focus, it doesn't matter what direction we take. This circle over here on the right represents our aspiration." I tap the board on the right circle, then tell the group that it represents what we strive to become. "If we know where we are today, the left circle, and we know what we want to become tomorrow, as represented by the right circle, we have a beacon to guide us. Without an aspiration, though, it doesn't matter which direction we take."

While stepping in the direction of Smoke's desk to address him, I remind him that earlier he said that he was only thinking about finishing his probation, then I asked whether he had any aspirations beyond his 21st birthday.

"I guess I'll find a job or something."

His answer lacks the force with which he spoke earlier, when he questioned me about prison credibility.

While erasing the line between the two dots on the blackboard I point out that probation ends for Smoke when he turns 21. Then I write the number 21 above the left circle. Above the right circle I write the number 31, and I tap the circle with my chalk while I address Smoke.

"Let's do an exercise in aspiring. Where would you like to see yourself when you're 31? If you could be all that you could be at 31, what would that mean to you? What would you like to be doing with your life? Think about it for a second, not something impossible, like a wish that you don't have control over. Imagine an aspiration you would like to pursue. What would that be?"

Smoke rests his chin on his hand while looking at me. "I never thought about it before. But you said you write books about prison. I wouldn't mind being a writer. I could write books that tell stories about what it's like growing up in the barrio."

"You could do anything you want," I assure him. "All it takes is the right attitude and an aspiration, a clearly defined goal. Have you read books about growing up in the barrio?"

"Not the barrio exactly, but I've read urban novels. They're the only kind of books I like reading. They describe street life, telling

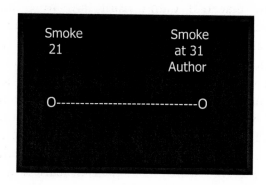

stories that I can get into. I could write about the barrio."

"You could write about aspiration you have." Above the right circle on the board, next to the number 31, I write the word Author. "If you want to advance from where you are at 21 to become an author at 31," I draw a new straight line between the two circles, "what steps do you think you would have to take in that direction?"

"I don't know," he laughs. "I've never written nothing before, nothing except what I had to write for class."

"That was the same position I was in when I was first locked in prison. I didn't know how to write a complete sentence, and I didn't know much about the rules of language. But I knew that if I didn't learn how to express myself in writing, I wouldn't ever be able to communicate beyond the walls of the penitentiary. My attitude was 100 percent. I wanted to learn how to write, and I'm still learning. In fact there may be millions of people who don't like what I write. But thankfully there are a few thousand who do. I write for them. You can do the same: write for a specific audience. So what does it take to learn how to write?"

"He has to stay in school," Lump says.

"Is that what you think, Smoke?" I ask. "Would you have to stay in school?"

"I guess. Get my GED, probably go to college."

"School became the answer for me," I said, "but I didn't realize it until I began serving this long sentence. I hated school when I was your age. But once I discovered my aspiration to be a writer, I approached my education with a completely different attitude. All of a sudden school wasn't something I had to do. Educating myself became like a ladder for me, and every assignment or course I completed was like climbing a step that would lead me out from the pit of confinement. If you aspire to become an author, learning to write becomes much more than a chore. You begin to *want* to learn, you empower yourself with your aspiration."

"But I wouldn't even know where to start." Smoke answers.

"That's not true," I counter. "When a person doesn't aspire to anything, that is when he doesn't know where to start. Nothing matters. Hopelessness and despair sets in because the person doesn't have any direction. But if you aspire to become an author, you acknowledge that you would need to continue with school. That's where I had to start. I wrote more than 1,000 words every day for longer than eight years and I read hundreds of books before I began to feel more confident as a writer. Writing takes work, practice, discipline. It's my attitude and aspiration that keeps me going. Believe me, my mentors and critics are always telling me that I need to improve, to work harder, to continue learning."

"What did you write about first?" Smoke asks.

"When I was learning I wrote about everything. After reading a book, I wrote about what I learned from the book. I wrote letters to people. I wrote stories about what I saw in prison, about what other prisoners told me about their experiences. You could be learning to write on a college campus, where you would have professors to guide you and help you learn. Since you wouldn't be learning to write in a concrete cell, learning probably wouldn't take you as long as it took me. But you still need the aspiration to keep you going, to keep a positive attitude. Picture your photograph on the cover of *Time* magazine in 10 years. Can you see it?"

"Yeah, right," Smoke laughs.

"There it is," I say, pointing to the imaginary magazine that I pretend to hold in my hand.

"Next to your picture is a headline inviting readers to learn more about Smoke, the bestselling author who used writing to transform himself from living a life of crime to become America's number one author of crime stories. He's a sensation, an inspiration to millions of young people, a chick magnet. Hollywood is basing blockbuster movies on his books. Can you see yourself in that role?"

"That would be nice." He's smiling.

"There isn't any reason you can't make it happen, Smoke. Be all that you can be. Have you seen the movie *Scarface*?"

"Like a hundred times."

"Well the guy who wrote the story was once exactly like you. He was a young man in a classroom who didn't know how to start. But he had an aspiration to become a writer. And he had an attitude that kept him on course. Do you know what the attitude and aspiration brought?"

"What?"

"Action!" I walk to the blackboard and draw a check beside the word representing the third step of the Straight-A Guide.

Action

Success! The Straight-A Guide

✓ Attitude
✓ Aspiration
✓ Action

"A*ttitude* is where everything begins," I reiterate while pointing to the first word in the Straight-A Guide, "because attitude empowers our will."

I move my finger lower and point to the second word listed on the blackboard.

"With a positive, confident attitude, our *aspiration* is for something better. Our attitude and our aspirations push us in the right direction. We need to stay conscious of each, using them to guide us through life like a GPS navigation system. But without *action*," I say referring to the third word listed on the blackboard, "we're stuck."

"You've got to have the will to succeed," Smoke begins to grasp the message.

"The will to succeed is only part of what's necessary. Do you know what's even more crucial than the will to succeed?" I ask, encouraging him to think about the next step.

"What's that?" Smoke doesn't venture a guess.

"Anyone?" I ask the class.

"You need the right attitude and aspiration," Trey says.

"That's true," I acknowledge, "but what's even more important than the will to succeed is the will to prepare. Our attitude and aspiration show us the path. They connect the dots from where we are now to where we want to go. As long as we follow that path, we will reach our aspiration, becoming what we want to become. It's one thing to know the path, but it's another to *walk* the path."

I pause to gesture toward the other prisoners who sit in chairs alongside the blackboard behind me.

"We're all at different stages and we're all pursuing our own aspirations. I've been marching along my path for longer than 23 years so my actions today are different from my actions at the beginning of my term. But every step is important as long as it advances me along the path to my aspiration."

I walk through the aisles of desks and continue talking to the students.

"I wasn't a good student in high school, so I knew I'd have to take many steps before I could become a writer. I had to study and work through numerous remedial courses before I could start taking college courses. But each of those courses was an action, a step along the path that would lead to my aspiration. Then I had to take action toward a college degree. Every assignment I completed in college advanced me another step forward. After graduating from college I had to take actions that would introduce me to the publishing world. Does anyone know how I did that from prison?"

"You sent letters out to introduce yourself," Lump ventures a guess.

"That would be one action step," I agree. "And what would happen, Lump, if I were to take the step of writing a letter?"

"The publisher would write you back, I guess."

"Maybe if I were someone famous," I laugh. "If I were as famous as Smoke is going to be in 10 years, then the publisher might write me back. But I'm a prisoner, a convicted drug offender, not a famous novelist, not a superstar. Writing one letter might be an action I could take, but that act alone wouldn't have been enough in my case. I had to take thousands of other steps and face many rejections before I advanced in noticeable ways.

"The will to succeed required the will to prepare. I made a 100-percent commitment to my aspiration, and that generated all the energy I needed to persevere. My aspiration to succeed made it possible to embrace rejection when it came.

"As an aspiring author, Smoke, could you keep a positive attitude, taking continuous action steps along your path even when confronted with countless rejections?"

"If you could do it, so could I."

"I'm with you," I agree with him. "There isn't anything you can't do, and if you commit to the Straight-A Guide I know that you can reach all of your aspirations. If you can see yourself as that best-selling author in years to come, then every action along the path toward that empowers you. Can you see how that approach differs from just trying to finish with probation, and then seeing what comes up later?"

"Well I wasn't thinking about being an author before," he laughs. "There isn't anyone writing books in my barrio."

"Maybe there is, maybe there isn't," I point out. "It doesn't matter what other people do; what matters is that you take clear, affirmative steps in the direction of your aspiration. And your aspirations don't have to require 10 years to become a reality. You're young and living in society. The limitations that block me and every other prisoner don't drag you down. What are some aspirations the rest of you could pursue?"

"I could see myself designing video games like *Grand Theft Auto*," Trey says.

"That's right, you could," I agree.

"I could build sick sound systems," Lump says with a gleam.

"I could become a businessman," Trey offers, "I'm good at selling stuff."

"How about others? Let's make a list of aspirations you could pursue."

I write student answers on the blackboard. When I finish, we have a list of 27 different occupations, from lifeguard to physician.

"What do all these aspirations have in common?" I ask.

"They're all jobs."

"Okay," I agree, "they're all jobs. But what does it take to qualify for such jobs?"

"The will to prepare," someone offers.

"That's right, and preparation requires action—small steps along the path. But as long as we keep our aspirations in focus, and pursue them with the right attitude, the action steps empower us. What are some actions that would be necessary for every occupation on the blackboard?"

"Finishing high school, and earning a diploma," another student calls out.

"Excellent answer," I agree, smiling. "A high school diploma or GED prepares you. It's a big step toward opening new opportunities. Just being in this classroom today is an action step each of you is taking toward your diploma, and if you see the high school credential as an action step on the way along the path to your aspiration, then the steps become empowering rather than burdensome. The steps become a part of your purpose."

I return to the blackboard and erase all of the occupations as I talk. "When I began serving my prison sentence, cars didn't come equipped with GPS navigation systems. The only place I've ever seen such systems were in advertisements. Can anyone tell me how a GPS works?"

"You mean how the electronics are wired?" Lump asks.

"No, that's way too complicated. I wouldn't understand that, but I know that anyone who designed and built them had to take numerous small steps before developing the end product. All I want you to tell me is how a GPS works. What happens when you turn it on?"

[85]

"In my dad's car the GPS comes on when you start the car," Lump explains. "If you want to find out how to get somewhere, you just put the address in and the GPS draws a map from where you are to where you're trying to go. It tells you how far away it is and how long it should take to get there, and it updates along the way. Then a cool blinking dot shows you exactly where you are and a voice comes on telling you where to turn."

"Does that GPS work pretty well in helping you reach your destination?" I ask.

"It's perfect," Lump responds. "Any fool can follow it and get where he's trying to go."

Accountability

Success! The Straight-A Guide

✓ Attitude
✓ Aspiration
✓ Action
✓ Accountability

I draw a check beside the next word in the Straight-A Guide: *accountability*.

"By holding ourselves accountable, we maintain a personal GPS system that guides us to our aspirations. The more precision we have in our systems of accountability, the less likely we are to fall off track."

From my pocket I pull out a blue vinyl book, about six inches long by three inches wide and I hold it up for the class to see. "Can anyone tell me what this is?"

"It's a checkbook," Trey guesses.

"It looks like a checkbook, doesn't it? But it's not." I flip through the pages so the class catches a glimpse of all the writing inside. "It's a weekly planner, part of my personal GPS system that I use to hold myself accountable."

"Why don't you use an electronic one, like an I-phone?" Smoke asks.

"Let's not forget that I'm a prisoner," I point out, grinning. "If you wear a prisoner's clothing, you won't have access to I-phones or any other fancy gadgets. But, even though we can't access fancy electronics, that doesn't mean we can't create our own accountability systems. This weekly planner is one of mine."

"What do you do?" Lump asks. "Write down what you plan on doing every week?"

"I use the weekly planner as one part of a more elaborate system that helps me stay on course," I explain. "Rather than using the small booklet to describe my future plans, I write brief notes that describe my daily progress. Pick a day," I tell the group," and I'll tell you what I wrote in my planner for that day."

"Any day?" Trey asks.

"Any day since the beginning of this year—I have a different book for each of the years I've served."

"What's it say for June 15, 2010?"

I flip to that page—a Tuesday—and read what I wrote in the small rectangular space. "In the left corner of the space, I wrote the numbers 8,345, 1:40, and 921."

"What do the numbers stand for?" Lump asks.

"The first number indicates the number of days I've served in prison. June 15 was my 8,345[th] day. The second number tells what time I woke that morning to begin my work. I started writing at 1:40 in the morning. The third number, 921, corresponds to an index I keep that identifies the daily blog that I wrote."

"I thought you said you don't have access to electronics," Smoke interrupts my description. "If you don't have electronics, how are you writing a daily blog?"

From my pocket I pull out a blue Bic pen. "With this," I hold up the pen for the class to see. "I write all of my work. I write with nothing more than a pen and a paper every day, and I send my work home through the mail. Then my wife coordinates the typing to post my blogs on the Web site she maintains on my behalf."

"You start you work at 1:40 in the morning." Lump looks incredulous. "That's the time I'm usually shutting down my video games to sleep."

"Remember a little while ago when I spoke about attitude?" I remind the class. "Attitude determines our level of commitment. The more commitment we invest into our aspirations, the more likely we'll reach them. We have to know our strengths and weaknesses. I'm a prisoner, but I'm 100 percent committed to reaching the goals I set. As a consequence to access to computers, I expect that I must work harder to do research and work longer to write with pen and paper. That's the action I must take. Waking early is part of the discipline, part of the way that I commit to making all of my aspirations more than dreams."

Then I continue reading in the square that defines my progress on June 15. It tells of the work I'm doing to complete a manuscript that describes a typical day for me in prison. I wrote through page 42, made copies of the work and mailed it home for my wife to type. I also wrote a blog on the subject of solitary confinement and the costs of imprisonment, and I wrote a love letter to my wife.

"At the bottom of the day's description," I show the group, "I wrote the progress I made towards my exercise goals. On June 15 I ran 10 miles, bringing my total running distance to 4,897 miles over the past 550 days. I followed the run with 800 pushups, bringing my total count of pushups for the year to 64,500."

"You even track your exercise?" Trey looks at me as if I'm unreasonable obsessive with my recordings of daily activities.

"As I said earlier, the daily planner is only part of my accountability system. At the beginning of each year I set clearly-defined, measurable goals and values, and I invite people to hold me accountable. With regard to exercise, my goal at the beginning of the year was to run more than 3,100 miles during the year and to do 100,000 pushups. Another goal this year was to write three manuscripts. All of my goals relate to the values that are essential to my life. My GPS system keeps me accountable."

"Keeping those records seems like a waste of time," Trey says. "You're writing all that stuff down in a booklet that no one but you is going to read. And since you're the one doing everything, you should already know how you're spending every day. I don't see how writing down everything you do gets you any closer to reaching your goals."

"Okay, maybe you're right."

I walk to the open space on the blackboard. "Let's test your theory. Trey, tell us what's different in your life today than from one year ago."

"I don't know," he laughs. "I'm another year older."

"That's true. You're another year older, but you didn't have anything to do with that. Can you tell us whether you made any changes that advanced you to the man that you want to become?"

"I'm closer to finishing high school. And I didn't have to write down every day what I did; all I had to do was come to school."

"Good point. You're closer to finishing school. Now, can you describe what you did yesterday?"

"Came to school, hung out, played some video games and listened to music. Stuff like that. Same thing I do every day."

After writing Trey's responses on the board, I draw a vertical line to create a separate column. "Now let's try something different. In Trey's column we have what he's doing. It's the usual routine—he wakes up in the morning and shows up for class. That's it. It doesn't take much thought. But what if Trey made the goals more clearly defined. What if he had an aspiration toward which he was striving, something specific? What was the aspiration you described earlier, Trey?"

"I said I'd like to design video games like *Grand Theft Auto.*"

I write Trey's aspiration on the board. "Okay. Tell us what you've done during the past year to make you a more likely candidate for a career as a video game designer."

"Like I said, I'm another year closer to graduating from high school."

"Can you think of anything else, something specific you might be able to do that would make it more likely for you to design games?"

"I don't know."

"Can anyone in the class think of what Trey might do to prepare for a career designing video games?"

"He has to go to college or a vocational school," Smoke helps.

I write the answer on the board.

"He could study computer programming," Lump offers.

"He could volunteer to work for a video game company as an apprentice." This is Smoke's second suggestion.

After writing the suggestions on the blackboard I ask Trey whether pursuing Smoke and Lump's suggestions would help or hurt his chances of designing video games.

"They'd help I guess," he shrugs, "but I still don't see how writing down everything I do would get me any closer to being a video game designer."

Awareness

> **Success! The Straight-A Guide**
> ✓ Attitude
> ✓ Aspiration
> ✓ Action
> ✓ Accountability
> ✓ Awareness

I place a check mark next to the word *awareness* on the blackboard. "That's because I haven't yet described the fifth step of the Straight-A Guide. Accountability mechanisms, our personal GPS systems, increase awareness of what we're doing to reach our aspirations. By clearly defining our values and goals with as much precision as possible, we give our lives direction."

I draw the two circles on the board again, one on the left side and another on the right side. "Remember that it's our objective to advance from one circle to the next, from where we are to where we want to be. Our accountability system keeps us moving in the right direction of our aspiration—where we want to be. But we also rely upon our GPS to increase awareness, first for ourselves, then for others."

I remind Trey that when I first asked him what distinguishes his life now from last year, all he could respond was that he was another year older and another year closer to finishing high school. His activities yesterday didn't show much of his commitment to his aspiration of designing video games.

"But you agree with Smoke and Lump that going to college, studying computer programming, and apprenticing for a video game designer might make you a better candidate for the career you'd like. Is that right?"

"Probably," Trey acknowledges.

"Okay, well your accountability system keeps you on track of what you're doing and the progress you're making. Not only that, it opens your eyes to other options that might move you closer to your aspirations. I call that increasing awareness. Some leaders in the business world refer to it as a SWOT plan." I write the letters on the board.

"You mean SWAT." Smoke corrects, mistakenly assuming I'm discussing the elite division of law enforcement.

"No, not SWAT," I assure him, "I mean SWOT. It stands for knowing our strengths, our weaknesses, our opportunities, and our threats. Like I said, it's all about keeping ourselves aware."

I explain to the group how—when I began serving my prison sentence—I aspired to reach society and connect with people outside by writing. With a 100 percent commitment to that goal, I considered all of my strengths and weaknesses, empowering my attitude with aspirations of transferring my life from simply serving time to becoming a person of relevance.

I lived with complete awareness of my surroundings and the awareness enabled me to make the most of opportunities and to navigate my way around threats. The aspirations inspired my every action. I didn't limit my interest to earning college degrees because pieces of paper that I could put in a frame were not going to sufficiently change my life. I needed to educate myself, to increase my knowledge, my skills, and my ability to communicate. I seized every opportunity.

When other prisoners or the system itself reminded me that I had decades yet to serve, I attributed the discouragement to a lack of awareness. The system would beat me over the head with the message that "Prisoners have nothing coming," but my attitude kept me advancing to my aspirations. The accountability system was a tool I could use to measure progress, and it trained me to seize opportunities that others missed. By using a precise accountability system I always understood where I was, how much further I had to go, and what more I could do to reach my aspiration. I was on a journey, charting my own course through imprisonment. Instead of emerging bitter and angry, I intended to lead a useful and productive life, with opportunities in abundance.

When I finish describing the ways that increasing awareness of my surroundings helped me, I stand in front of the class and ask a question. "Besides expanding my own awareness, do you know what else my accountability system does?"

No one ventures a guess, but I see that I have the group's attention.

"It builds awareness in others. When I write out the values and goals that I commit to pursuing, I simultaneously invite others to hold me accountable. Then, as I track my progress with daily updates, I keep the world up to day with what I'm doing and how I'm doing it. Those actions show discipline and they inspire others to cheer me on, to become supportive, to lend a hand. Using an accountability system to measure my actions keeps me constantly aware of the importance of always striving to do more. I can see how you can do the same, Trey. Can you?"

"What? Like going to college, studying computer programming? I can see how that would help me become a game designer."

"But you can take smaller steps, and by doing so you can increase both your own awareness and an awareness in others. If you create opportunities to bring mentors into your life, you will strengthen yourself, as they will develop a vested interest in helping you reach your aspirations—even the little ones."

"Like what? Whaddaya mean?"

I walk back to the blackboard where I wrote the descriptions of college, computer programming, and apprenticing suggestions that Lump and Smoke offered.

"I would call these major goals or action plans on your way to becoming a video game designer. Do you know why?"

"Because I haven't finished high school yet," Trey says, shrugging.

"You're on the way to finishing high school, and that's a good start. But do you know anything about college?"

"I've never been to one."

"Then one step you could take to increase your awareness would be to research colleges. What's a smaller step that would lead to increasing your awareness? You could figure out what colleges offer the best training for video game developers. Then you could figure out what courses you need to master in order to qualify for the school, and what barriers might exist to entry. If you make yourself aware of all that is necessary to begin a career as a video game designer, then you move closer to reaching your aspiration."

"But how does researching colleges make others aware of me," Trey asks, "or want to support me?"

"Because by researching the schools that interest you, you may also discover which professors teach the courses that you want to study. You could write them letters to introduce yourself and express your desire to learn from them. You could call them and maybe even go visit them."

"What if the professor doesn't write back?"

"Then you write again, or you write another one. Finding a suitable mentor could become part of your action plan. Think of yourself on a boat in the ocean. If you don't cast a line you won't catch any fish. If you cast one line, at least you have a chance. But if you cast one hundred lines, or one thousand lines, won't you increase your chances of catching a fish?"

Trey smiles.

"The more efforts you make to reach out, the more chances you have of finding others who will help you. That's what the Straight-A Guide is all about. You can use it as a tool, consulting it regularly to keep aware of every opportunity to advance closer to your goal. By refining your accountability system, you always know where you are and whether you're using time and resources to the best of your ability, measuring your progress every day."

"What if after researching the colleges I find out that it's too expensive and I can't afford it?"

"Well the world needs ditch diggers too." The class laughs. "Would you like to dig ditches for a living?"

"I'm not digging any ditches."

"Then how about washing dishes? Do you like kitchen duty, scrubbing pots and pans?"

"No."

"Then I suggest you consult your Straight-A Guide, because if you use it wisely, it will lead you to all the resources you need to reach your aspirations. But you won't reach them by accident. Reaching your aspiration requires 100 percent commitment, action, and accountability. If you commit yourself with discipline, making more people aware by the ways that you distinguish yourself from the dreamers, you will create your own path. You'll find scholarships and support, but you have to cast your lines. Can you do that?"

"Yup," Trey answers with confidence.

"Okay," I challenge him.

"Then tell me some other lines you can cast. I suggested researching colleges and writing professors. What else could you do to increase your awareness and the awareness of others?"

Trey hesitates. Finally he says, "You're putting me on the spot. I need time to think about it."

"Can we get some help?" I ask the class.

"Just like researching colleges," Smoke says, "he could go to the library and research the books available on game design, and he could research companies in the area that design video games. Then he could write to the people who wrote the books, or go volunteer to apprentice at the companies."

"Bingo!"

I'm hopeful that others in the class see how to use the Straight-A Guide as well as Smoke intuitively has.

"The more lines he casts, the more he becomes aware of what he can do to catch his fish. And every action he takes leads him closer to his aspiration."

Achievement

Success! The Straight-A Guide

- ✓ Attitude
- ✓ Aspiration
- ✓ Action
- ✓ Accountability
- ✓ Awareness
- ✓ Achievement

I return to the numerated list of the Straight-A Guide and draw a check next to achievement, the sixth step.

"When we set our eyes on major aspirations, like becoming a video game designer, or like Smoke's becoming a best-selling author of books that describe life in the barrio, we need to celebrate every achievement along the way. Celebrating our achievements keeps our attitude strong, helping us maintain our commitment to reaching our aspirations.

"Smoke, can you describe some achievements you might want to celebrate on the path to becoming a best-selling author?"

"I'd celebrate when I finished writing my first book."

"I'm sure the whole class would join me in celebrating with you when you finished writing your first book," I assure him. "But can you imagine all the smaller steps you're going to take before you finish writing that book? You're going to strengthen yourself if you can celebrate each of those little steps because they all move you closer to what you're aspiring to become."

"Like what? What little steps should I celebrate?"

"Do you want to know one achievement of yours that I'm celebrating right now?"

He laughs.

"When I walked in here I felt the skepticism like a dark cloud."

I turn to the group of prisoners who have been waiting patiently for their turn to speak.

"Did you guys feel it?"

"It was dark brother," Julius answers. He is serving 10 years for his crimes and I look forward to listening to his powerful message that he'll share with the students.

"That's right it was dark. And Smoke, you struck me as being the most skeptical of the group, judging us before we spoke as if we were another group of do-gooders coming to preach to you."

He laughed.

"Your face was hard, grimacing, and I didn't know whether any of us would be able to convince you of a better way. When I asked about your plans, you expressed hopelessness and cynicism. Now you can see a teeny bright, hopeful spot. The choices you make will determine what you become. I'm celebrating that you can see your own potential—your face on the cover of *Time* as a best-selling author who shows the world what it's like to grow up in the barrio."

"But I haven't done that yet."

"You may not have written your first book, but we can celebrate the change in your attitude. At least you see yourself as something more than the circumstances that surround you. That's a start. That's an achievement. If you can keep that aspiration alive, you will take the next step, and then the step after that. I want you to celebrate every step because every step is an achievement; one that brings you closer to your aspirations."

"How are we supposed to celebrate?" Trey asks. "What does that mean…to have a party, to holler and scream with joy?"

"You need to find internal ways to celebrate, to reward yourself," I say, pausing for a moment to remember the rewards I've given myself over the years. I pull out my day timer from my pocket again.

"I'm a great list maker. Every day I write lists of what I'm working toward and the incremental progress I make. I find ways to celebrate the little successes. Even now I record every mile I run, and every pushup. But I've been exercising for so long that it's a part of my life, no different from brushing my teeth. So it wouldn't make sense to celebrate every mile. Rather every mile represents another step I'm taking toward release, and every time I reach a 500-mile increment, I celebrate with a meal of nachos that I share with my roommate. You've got to celebrate your achievements to keep the aspiration alive, I think. Figure out how you can reward yourself. I can think of ways that might work."

"Like what?"

"When I asked what you did yesterday, you said that you spent time playing video games and listening to music," I remind Trey.

"That's right."

"If you use the Straight-A Guide to lead you to a career as a video game designer, you might question the level of commitment you're making. By looking at your accountability tools, your personal GPS, you could measure how much time you're devoting to preparing. Instead of sliding through each day without making measurable progress toward the goals you set, you could discipline yourself. As I deny myself nachos until I run a 500-mile increment, you could deny yourself playing a video game until you read one book on video game design."

Trey frowns, as if I suggested he clean out the garage. "What if playing video games is part of my research?"

"It may be part of your research," I respond over the laughter of the class. "You are charting your own course, and you can rely on the Straight-A Guide to determine whether you're allocating your time wisely. Maybe you can celebrate by playing a game every time you read a chapter, or even a page. You decide. The choices you make will either bring you closer to your aspirations or they will threaten your progress. You're the captain of your own ship, and what's important is that you know the way to reach your destination. Finding ways to celebrate the small achievements you make may help you stay the course."

I return to the blackboard and draw a check beside the final step in the Straight-A Guide, next to the word "appreciation."

Appreciation

> ## Success! The Straight-A Guide
>
> ✓ Attitude
> ✓ Aspiration
> ✓ Action
> ✓ Accountability
> ✓ Awareness
> ✓ Achievement
> ✓ Appreciation

"More than describing something we do, the last step represents a way of interpreting the events of our life, and I hope I can explain it adequately. By living in accordance with the Straight-A Guide, what we're really doing is living a values-centered life and identifying what's important to us with our attitudes and aspirations. The guide helps us stay the course, to do what we say we're going to do.

"In living this way through so many years, I've found that it brings an appreciative state of mind. Rather than living with a sense of entitlement, as I did before I came to prison, the Straight-A Guide helps me realize that I have duties and responsibilities. We all do. And when we strive to prove worthy of and appreciate the blessings and opportunities that come our way, we invite more blessings and opportunities into our lives. That's why it's important to live with gratitude for all we receive."

"You've got to be kidding," Smoke says. "So do you appreciate the 45-year sentence your judge hit you with?"

"Would you believe me if I told you that I did?"

"No."

"It's true. I am grateful—for *all* of the blessings of my life. That appreciation is the reason I can stand before you during my 24th year of imprisonment, knowing that I expect to serve three more years, without any bitterness or anger inside of me. Prison has been a part of my journey, but it doesn't define me. By living in accordance with the Straight-A Guide I will emerge from prison stronger than when I walked in. Whatever challenges that you and your classmates may face, if you embrace the Straight-A Guide, I know that each of you can do the same. So aim high."

Chapter Four

Julius Lige:
Growing Up on the Streets of
East Oakland

I appreciate the students' attention and the questions and comments from Smoke, Lump, and Trey. I know that my credibility with them is rooted in the length of time I've served, but the other speakers have a different sort of credibility. They grew up amidst the same kinds of chaos as many students in the class. When Julius stands his powerful build alone is enough to grab the class's attention.

"I'm glad everyone in the class had a chance to listen to my man Mike describe what he calls the Straight-A Guide," Julius begins, pacing in front of the students desks as he talks. Julius limps slightly because of nerve damage from old gunshot wounds.

Success!
The Straight-A Guide
✓ Attitude
✓ Aspiration
✓ Action

Julius references the blackboard. "You can call the guide whatever you want, but I relate to the importance of attitude, and aspirations, and action."

"When I was your age, my attitude, aspirations and actions were different from the way they are now. Back then I was battlin' on the wild streets of East Oakland, one of the murder capitals of the world. I grew up knowin' what it's like to dodge bullets, to hustle, because that's what I was about. But I also know that if I'd had a different attitude when I was growin' up, I wouldn't be losin' 10 years in the bing right now."

"Where you was from in East Oakland?" a young man asks. His hair is tightly wrapped in cornrows, and a gold-capped front tooth shines in his mouth.

"Do you know somethin' about the Bay area?" Julius asks the student.

"My peoples is from there."

"What's your name pahtner?" Julius walks toward the student.

"I'm Andre," he says. "They call me Dre."

Julius establishes a rapport by bumping fists with the student, then tells him where he grew up. "They call it the murder dubs now," Julius says, "but back then the neighborhood was known as the 20s. I went to Manzanita elementary school, then to Roosevelt Junior High."

"I went to Roosevelt," Dre says.

"Then you know what I'm talkin' about."

Julius tells the class what it was like. "All my pahtners and I grew up diggin' the hustlers who were flossin', pushin' Caddies and Benzes, slingin' dope. We had the attitude of wantin' to be just like them. Because of that attitude, we stood ready to do whatever it took to come up."

Dre and several of his classmates are nodding in agreement, identifying with his descriptions of neighborhood influences.

"You know what my attitude was about because you're living it right now, but who can tell me what my aspirations were back then?"

Several hands go up in response to Julius's question and he calls on a young man who had so far remained silent. The student had shaved his head and he wore a plaid flannel shirt buttoned to the top.

"You was wanting to be the big baller."

"That's what's up," Julius acknowledges and asks the student his name.

"Jamal," the student answers.

"You're right, Jamal. I wanted to be the big baller, the dope man. So tell me, Jamal," Julius walks back to the blackboard, pointing to the Straight-A Guide, "What actions did I have to take if I was setting out to become the big baller?"

"You had to hustle that work."

Again the class laughs. They know what that means.

"That's right. And now I stand in front of you so you can see what it got me. I been kidnapped, held at gun point, and shot at. Now I'm locked up, separated from my wife and kids. That's what I'm here to talk about, hoping that all my young pahtners will listen and make better decisions with better attitudes, higher aspirations, and more disciplined actions than I chose.

"I didn't have to become another statistic, another black man in prison. I had plenty of chances. You all know what I'm talking about because you're there right now, living in the same kinds of streets I was in with all the same pressures. There's always a way out, but no one finds it without the right attitude. At least I didn't."

Julius walks back toward Dre and asks why the young man isn't attending school in Oakland if that's where his family lives.

"I got locked up in juvie for robbery. When I got out my moms thought a change would do me good. She sent me down here to live with my uncle. Then I caught a case for selling weed and part of my probation means I got to finish this alternative school."

"That's exactly what I'm talkin' about, and you ain't alone," Julius is talking to the entire class now. "Our prisons are filled with cats who're living that same story. I'm one of 'em. Those of us in prison are just a few chapters deeper into the story than you cats are right now. My moms did the same thing, moving our family from where we was staying in the 20s to a better area so I could attend Skyline High School. You know where Skyline's at?" Julius asks Dre.

"It's up by Oakland Hills, right?"

Julius describes the significance of the move. His mother worked 12-hour days for the city and didn't bring home a huge paycheck, but she was making sacrifices to give Julius and his brother a better environment. Like Dre, Julius says he was getting involved in crime and spent some time in Juvenile Hall. The move to the Skyline neighborhood was supposed to transport Julius away from the bad influences of

the notorious 20s blocks and into a more family-oriented neighborhood. Skyline High School had an excellent football program, with top-tier universities sending scouts regularly to recruit, and some students went on to careers in the NFL. As an explosive linebacker with both speed and size, Julius had opportunities.

[119]

"The football career was waitin' for me, but my attitude wasn't in it. At least not 100 percent the way it was supposed to be. During the season I was on top of my game, leading the defense with quarterback sacks, but who can tell me where I was when practice ended?"

"Out hustlin'," Jamal guesses. "Movin' that work."

"That's what's up," Julius agrees. "I loved football, but I also loved the action of the streets. I didn't have that 100 percent attitude Mike was talking about, like it says here on the board. Without the right attitude, I didn't have any real aspirations of moving on to the NFL, my dreams weren't nothin' more than fantasies. An aspiration takes commitment and that commitment begins with a 100-percent attitude of doin' right. My Moms may have made every sacrifice to move me to a better neighborhood, just like your peoples is doin' for you Dre, but without the right attitude, the move didn't do no good for me. I was packin' my attitude from the rollin' 20s with me, bringin' crime to the new neighborhood. You can see where it got me."

Julius calls on Jamal who asks how Julius got shot.

"You know, packin' heat and gunshots ain't nothing' new. Look at the blackboard." Julius lists the Straight-A Guide. "You got attitude, aspirations, action, accountability, awareness, achievement, and appreciation. The Straight-A Guide doesn't only work in a positive sense. Same thing make you laugh can make you cry. I was a hustler, doin' whatever I had to do to come up in the streets, and I made a name for myself. What happens when your name starts ringin' bells?"

"Everyone knows you're the man," Smoke asserts.

"That's right. I create that awareness all around from my actions. By slingin' that dope, people started to figure I was getting' that paper. And what happened next? I wasn't findin' the positive people Mike was talkin' about who were out to help me succeed. I was in the streets, doin' dirt. Didn't take long for some of the OGs to come at me, tryin' to take me out the game, stick me for my paper. As I said before, I been kidnapped, held at gun point, sometimes cats came at me dumpin' bullets, and I caught a few bullets. That's what ended my football career."

"But we ain't all football stars," Dre points out. "Some of us knows we ain't going to the NFL."

"I hear that," Julius responds, "and I'm not tryin' to say that you are. But every player in this room has choices to make. Consequences are going to follow those choices, and everyone would be better off realizin' those choices now—before the serious trouble comes down on you. Believe me, anyone can get it."

Julius tells the class how it wasn't only football that gave him an opportunity for a better life. His father died when he was only 11, but he left opportunities for Julius to pursue a career as a union longshoreman, an opportunity Julius says would have provided excellent earnings and stability. Yet his attitude caused him to ignore some positive opportunities.

"Don't mistake me for no fool," Julius tells the class, "and don't play yourself. You can go around tellin' others you don't have any options, but I'm not the one to hear it. I know better because I was there. Ever' man in this room has options."

Julius walks over to a bookshelf and pulls out a math book.

"Tell me, Jamal, what's two plus three?"

Jamal shrugs, laughs off Julius's question.

"You think I'm playin' with you? Either you know or you don't!"

"It's five," comes the sullen response.

"That's right, it's five. You see how easily Jamal answered that! Is there anyone in this room who doesn't know that two plus three equals five?"

No student raises a hand.

"Okay," Julius makes his point, "just as easily as ever'one here knows that two plus three equals five, if you have the right attitude you can work to understand every one of the problems in this math book. You can understand algebra, geometry, even trigonometry if you can see what other options that knowledge will open for you. Don't be a fool like so many of us in prison were. You got to take advantage of the opportunities openin' up for you now, before these people lock you up in a cell, where nothin' matters but the turnin' of calendar pages."

Julius tells the group that he is serving a 10-year sentence, but he knows the sentence he received was a stroke of good fortune. In making the choices he made when he was the same age as the students in the class, he says that a judge easily could have slammed him with a life sentence.

"When I was out in the streets I used to fool myself with that same kind of nonsense 'bout there not bein' any opportunities. Truth is," Julius acknowledges, "it wasn't until I was locked up that I could look back with clarity and see all the opportunities I let slide by. I ignored them because I didn't have the right attitude. My teachers wanted to help me, my coaches wanted to help me, my mom wanted to help me, even my girl friend wanted to help me. But I didn't want to help myself. I was stuck in the game, and I was lucky to get out with only a 10 piece. I got a grip a pahtners servin' all day, life without parole, and I know too many cats who lost their lives to bullet holes. Truth is, prison may have saved me, but I should've learned these lessons when I was your age. You don't have to learn them in a prison cell. It all starts with changin' to a positive attitude."

Julius begins telling the students how prison changed his attitude by asking a question. "How many of you think you're ready to serve 20 years, 30 years, or life?"

"I ain't tryin' to do no time like that," Jamal says.

"No one is, but too many of us brothers out there makin' decisions that lead to the penitentiary or to the cemetery. When I was sweatin' out worries in the jail, wonderin' what type of time I was facing, I had an attitude change. My pahtner in the cell beside me just got slammed with a 30-year bid and I didn't want no part of it. More important than that, I saw the light and realized I had to change my attitude, to change everythin' about the way I was livin'. That's what being a man is all about."

Julius describes how he made the decision to change his life, not only for himself, but for the wife and children who love and support him. "My family is everything to me, and I'm determined to walk out from this prison term as the best man I can be. I should've made that commitment before, but it's never too late to start doin' right. I couldn't see myself puttin' my family through all that stress again, and so while I was locked in that jail cell, I made that commitment to leave the life of hustlin' behind once and for all. I made the 100 percent commitment to walk out from prison as a better man, a better husband, father, son, and leader. That's what I'm about now, and every step I take leads me closer to that vision."

With a clear vision in mind of how he wanted to emerge, he knew the actions he would have to take. They began with a step-by-step plan to lose weight.

"When I began servin' this sentence I was tippin' the scales at 325 pounds."

"No way," Dre couldn't believe that the athletic looking man standing in front of him used to be obese.

"I'm not playin'," Julius says. He pulls out a picture that shows the class what he looked like before his attitude change, and passes it around. "I've shed more than 100 pounds since I was locked up, and it didn't happen by accident. Who can tell me how I did it?"

"By dieting and exercise," comes the response from Lump, mimicking a TV ad.

"Those were the actions I took, but I began by changin' my attitude. I made a 100 percent commitment to leadin' a clean, healthy life, and losin' weight was one of the goals I set. I could envision myself back in top physical condition, and like the board says, I took action, holdin' myself accountable."

Julius couldn't walk one lap around the track without having to stop for a rest when he arrived at the prison. He tells the group how he kept pushing himself, and how he keeps pushing himself, exercising for three and sometimes four hours every day.

"That's the kind of discipline and commitment I should've begun applyin' to my life when I was your age. But I didn't. My attitude wasn't right back then. I kept makin' decisions without considering where those decisions would eventually lead me. And you all know where hustlin' leads? No hustler wants to answer that question when he's clockin' dollars in the street, puttin' in work, but it all leads either to the penitentiary or the cemetery. That's it!"

"What you got left to serve?" asks a student who has been sitting quietly all morning, listening but not interacting. The sleeves of his sweatshirt are pushed up. On the inside of his forearms I see familiar horizontal welts that healed badly from razor slashes.

"I've got about three, maybe four years left," Julius answers.

"So that's it? You just gonna work out for three more years?"

"What's your name, pahtner?"

"Jay."

"Check it, Jay," Julius talks while walking back to the blackboard. "This Straight-A Guide here, it's not like that. It's not about a

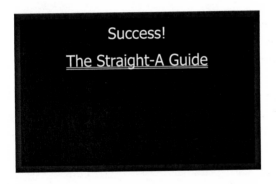

single dimension, but about a life plan. I didn't have a plan before I was locked down, but ever'thin' I'm doing with my life now relates to the aspirations I had when this sentence ends and I return to my community."

"When my sentence ends I'm goin' to work to make communities better, providin' the type of leadership that will show young people the lessons I learned. I need to do all I can to prepare for that role, sharin' my story like I'm doin' here through these prison outreach programs. When I'm home I'll have the liberty to spend more than one day in community schools, and I'm confident that I'll put programs together that make a difference in people's lives. That's what I'm workin' toward."

"Hold up," Smoke holds his hands up in a 'time out.' "You're out here talking to us from the prison while you're serving time, when you don't need no money. How do you think you'll be able to do this when you get out if there isn't any money to pay you?"

"That's a good question, Smoke, but it isn't a question I have the answers to right now. I've learned that I don't have to start with all the answers. What I have to start with is 'what.' Who can answer that?"

"You've got to have the right attitude," Lump says.

"You're dead right, pahtner. You've got to start with the right attitude and an aspiration. My aspiration isn't to make money, but to make a difference in people's lives. That's what I'm about." Julius points to the third A on the board. "What actions do I have to take to reach my aspirations?"

"Lose weight," someone offers.

Julius laughs. "What do you want me to do, fade away? I'm weighin' 215 right now. That's my prime fightin' weight."

To drive home the point Julius does some quick shadow boxing for the class with lightning speed.

"What else do I have to do?"

"Watch your diet?" Trey guesses.

"Come on fellas." Julius taps two fingers to his temple. "I've got to strengthen my mind. See what I've got here?"

With that, he opens a folder and proudly holds up a copy of his college degree.

"Some people serve time in prison, but I pride myself on doing' more. This college degree isn't the end of my education, but the start, part of my action plan. I hold myself accountable by readin' at least one book every month and writin' about what I'm learnin'. By the time I finish this prison sentence, I'll be much more prepared to contribute to my community, and just as I'm advisin' you, I'll be usin' the Straight-A Guide to reach the goals I set."

Julius gives some concluding remarks and thanks the class for their courtesy and attention. Before sitting down, he introduces Kenny Lumpkin, the most senior member and leader of our prison youth outreach program.

Chapter Five

Kenny Lumpkin:
A Tale from Watts

In his early 40s, Kenny Lumpkin walks with the relaxed, easy confidence of a middle-aged athlete. For the past 14 years he has been living in various federal prisons. He's the homerun hitting champion in the prison, but his passion centers on delivering positive messages to the young offenders and at-risk adolescents our prison outreach group tries to connect with and advise.

"How're you guys doing this morning?" By now the class is comfortably with us. The young men receive Kenny with an openness that I didn't feel until the *end* of my discussion.

"I've been sitting here watching, studying your faces and gauging your level of interest since we first walked in. I'm familiar with the schools and detention centers where you guys spend your teens, your early 20s, because I've been coming out to speak in these kinds of places for the past several years. It's always a challenge for me to figure out ways to connect, to send a message that's going to reach you now, before you're in deeper, locked inside a prison somewhere."

The students eye Kenny closely, evaluating his authenticity, just as they did with

Julius and me, but I sense that they're more receptive now.

"Do any of you feel like you're in prison right now?"

No one in the class raises his hand.

"No one has even the slightest feeling of being locked up?" Kenny asks skeptically. "You all know it's not normal to attend school under the watchful eye of a man with a gun, don't you?"

The officer has been sitting on his chair observing, chewing gum silently for the past hour, allowing the students to interact more freely than at first.

"Might not be a normal school," Trey admits, "but everyone here has at least some free time. Even those of us who return to juvie after school have a few hours to ourselves before lockdown."

Kenny nods as he takes in Trey's comment.

"The reason I bring it up is because you're a lot closer to prison than you may realize. Being in a school like this is kind of a wake-up call, and it's unfortunate that too many miss the signs before it's too late. I had a similar wake-up call before my judge slammed me with

20 years, but I wasn't paying attention. I thought I could keep doing what I was doing without ever facing any real punishment."

"What did you get a 20 piece for?" Smoke asks.

"Selling a few grams of crack."

The class lets out a collective gasp, amazed at the length of time Kenny received for his crime.

"You must've done something more than sell a few grams of crack to catch a 20-year sentence," Jamal insists. "My brother sold crack and he only got 10 years."

"You say 10 years as if it's nothing more than a bag of stale popcorn. Do you have any idea what it's like to serve 10 years?"

"I know a 10-year sentence would be easier to serve than 20 years," Jamal answers. "I know that much."

"You've got that right. Do you want to know why I'm serving 20 years instead of 10 years?"

"You must've got caught with a gun," Jay guesses. "I hears judges give longer sentences to dealers packing heat."

"They do," Kenny agrees. "But I didn't have a gun. What I did have was a wake-up call that I didn't pay attention to. Just like everyone in this class, I was charged with a crime and given a chance to straighten out my life. In your case, on account of your age, the judge gave probation, or maybe some time in juvenile hall, or whatever. I was in my early 20s the first time I got stung in a drug case, but my judge gave me straight probation. That was my wake-up call. I didn't take it seriously, kept myself in the game. When I got busted a second time for selling crack, the law required that the judge give me 20 years—double the sentence I would've received if I hadn't had a previous criminal record. And guess what? If any of you are ever convicted of a drug case, the criminal record that results in your being in this classroom is going to come back to haunt you. The judge who sentences you is going to slam you, just as my judge slammed me. On account of your having a prior criminal record, the judge will double the years that you otherwise would've received. I'm not saying this to scare you, but to give you a heads up. I didn't know about 'enhanced sentences' before, but I wish I would have known. I'm here to share a message of what's waiting for those who persist with crime."

"They can't double our sentences," Smoke offers his interpretation of the law. "All of us were convicted as juveniles. Our records won't count against us as adults."

"Is that the wisdom you picked up from the homies?"

"Everybody knows that," Smoke challenges, but he doesn't sound as sure of himself as he did a minute ago.

Kenny looks back at those of us who sit in the chairs beside the blackboards and grins, making eye contact with Osvaldo, a young prisoner who will describe a more accurate version of the law when it's his turn to speak.

"Check it out, Smoke," Kenny says. "I know I stand up here looking old enough to be your father, but try not to think of me as someone who's talking *at* you. I relate to where you're coming from. You said earlier that you've been trapped in the system since you were 13. In a few months you'll turn 21 and you want to be finished with it. But I've got a story to tell. For people like us, the system never forgets or forgives. I'm still locked inside and all I can do is share what I know. If you listen, you might find more reasons to make decisions that will keep you from coming inside, because you don't want anything like what I'm living."

"When you say people like us," Jamal interrupts, "what do you mean by that?"

"I'm talking about people who grow up in hard times, without influential parents to guide them, without neighborhood role models or mentors who show them how to fit in to society without having to detour through schools like this."

"Was that how you grew up?" Smoke asks.

"Brother I've been a prisoner all my life," Kenny answers. "I came out of the womb a prisoner of poverty. My biological parents were so poor they didn't even want me, put me up for adoption before I even knew who they were. I was adopted into a mixed-racial family; my mom was Mexican, my dad was black but he abandoned us by the time I was three, leaving me to raise myself on the streets."

"What do you mean raise yourself?"

"My mom was home," Kenny says, "but she was passed out or high on pills and alcohol a lot of the time. I love her to death, but I couldn't understand that she was stuck in her own prison of poverty, living on welfare in a run-down place with the lights always off. As a little kid I couldn't understand that, and I felt better hanging out in the streets, where I found every bad influence in the world. To me, there wasn't anything wrong with stealing, hustling dope, gang banging. That was all I knew from the time I could walk. Can any of you relate to a childhood like that?"

I try to count all the hands that go up in response to Kenny's question, but I lose track at a dozen before Kenny continues.

"I grew up in Watts in the Grape Street projects. Do any of you know where that is?"

Another show of hands.

"I went to 102nd Street Elementary, to Markham Junior High, and to Jordon High School. When I say the prison system is built for people like us, what I'm talking about are people who grew up in areas like mine, where kids look up to the dope dealers and gang leaders. That's all I wanted to be since I was five or six. All I wanted was a wad of cash in my pocket, flashy whips and hot chicks. The only ways I thought I could get it were either through hustling or playing ball. Truth is I was more of a jock growing up than a hustler," Kenny refers back to the blackboard, "but I wasn't feeling the Straight-A plan as a youngster. No one ever walked me through the reasons I needed to look beyond what I was doing in the moment. That's the reason I've been locked up for the past 14 years, and it's the reason I'm standing up here talking to you today."

"What sports did you play?" Jay asks.

"Everything, anything with a ball, but baseball was my game. If I had the right attitude, I might've even made a career of it. I played in the minor leagues for both the Chicago White Sox and the Kansas City Royals. But my commitment wasn't all there, and I never advanced to the point where I could earn any real money. So what do you think I did?"

"You had to do what you had to do," Trey explains. "You hustled that work."

"You're partly right. I made some money selling weed and crack. But it wasn't what I *had to do*," he emphasized. "It was the only thing I knew *how to do*. I was a father before I finished high school and I needed to make some money for my baby's momma. I've never held a job; wouldn't have even known where to go about getting one. All I knew was baseball and the streets. I didn't know anything about these words on the board: attitude, aspirations, actions, and all that."

"So if you could do it over again," Jamal asks, "would you focus more on playing ball?"

"Now that I'm older, and since I've watched the world pass me by while I live locked in one prison or another, I see everything differently. You have to understand, I know what it's like to lose. By the time I came to prison I was the father of five kids, and all of them grew up without me being home for them. It's not easy going through life trying to parent through a long-distance telephone call, not seeing family. I've gone through years with the only human touch that I've known has been the feel of a guard's hands on my wrists while he is locking them in steel cuffs behind my back. So any of you want to live like that?"

Students in the class mumble, fidgeting as they each object to the portrait Kenny paints of long-term imprisonment.

"Gates slammed me shut in a cell with nothing more than a steel toilet and my thoughts. Let me tell you, when a man lives

locked up like that for years at a time he has every kind of thought imaginable. I used to wonder if it would ever end, and I used to wonder what I could've done differently with my life so I wouldn't have had to lose so much. I needed to build my life on something more solid than a fantasy."

Kenny talks with the class about how every boy in the projects grows up with dreams of playing in the major leagues, in the NFL, or the NBA. Then he points out how tough it is for a kid to make it as a professional athlete.

"And when you come from the projects, the only way out besides sports is through hustling—at least that was what I saw then. Now I'm older and the scars I'm living with help me see more. It's what I'm hoping to show you before you make the same bad decisions that I made."

"I know what you're trying to show us," Jamal says.

"Okay. If you know so much, tell me what I'm trying to show you."

"That we need to stay in school," he grins.

"You got that right," Kenny nods. But that isn't my only message. What I want you to see is that you can grow into anything you want to become. You see, I've been where you are and I know what's in your heart. You live in a world that tells you, 'you ain't nothin' but bad'."

Kenny turns to the officer and in an aside says that he doesn't mean any disrespect but he wants to speak frankly with the class. The officer nods in assent.

"It isn't normal to grow up in foster homes, in juvenile hall, in trouble with the law. But none of you are bad kids, you just aren't growing up with the role models who encourage you to reach your potential. People who grow up in neighborhoods like Grape Street in Watts or other projects aren't afraid of prison because everyone they know has been locked up at one time or another, and every kid knows that it's only a matter of time before he's standing up for count. I'm here to tell you it doesn't have to be like that. It didn't have to be like that for me, and it doesn't have to be like that for you. You just have to believe in yourself, even if nobody else does. You need to 'check yourself before you wreck yourself,' like the song says."

The class laughs.

"I like all the guidance you can find in these words here," Kenny refers to the Straight-A Guide, "and Mike explained what he means by each of them. But I've got several words I want to share with you, even if they don't start with the letter 'a'. Can anyone tell me what integrity means?"

No one in the class raises his hand and Kenny looks over at me. "How about you, Mike. What does integrity mean?"

"Integrity describes when a person holds himself together, keeping his values in line with his actions."

"That's what I'm talking about," Kenny acknowledges. "Integrity might not start with the letter 'a', but that's a word I want you to think about. I think it was Julius who asked you earlier if anyone was ready to serve 10 years in prison, and not one of you raised your hand. But what are you doing with your lives? Are you making decisions with the attitude of doing right, or making something more of your life? Or are you making the kinds of decisions that are going to bring you into trouble with the law? You've already been labeled by this system as a delinquent, and those felonies you're packing won't ever be ignored. If you don't want to lose all your birthdays and holidays to a concrete cell, then I suggest you hold yourself accountable, that you make yourself aware of where the decisions you're making are bound to lead. If you're making decisions that lead to a better life, then you're making decisions with integrity. If not, then you're just playing

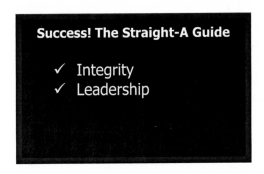

yourself, even if you might not know it."

Kenny walks to the blackboard and writes the word *integrity*, then he tells the class that he has two other words he wants to add, and he writes down the first one: *leadership*.

"Leadership doesn't start with the letter 'a' either, but it's important for you to understand. What does leadership mean to you, Smoke?"

He shrugs. "Isn't it obvious? It means to lead, not to follow."

"I'd like to believe that the meaning of leadership is obvious, but as a prisoner I'm always looking around and seeing how few of my brothers really understand what it means. You see, in prison you can be sure that everyone says that he's going to make it when he gets out. But prisons are all about conditioning people to fail. The people who run prisons say they want prisoners to be responsible, but then they take away all sense of responsibility. They say they want prisoners to live positively and constructively, but the system degrades men and makes them useless. They say they want prisoners to develop self-worth, but the prison doesn't do anything but destroy a man's self-worth. The only way to triumph over such conditions is to exercise leadership, a man has to lead himself. Prisoners may say they know the way to prepare for the obstacles they're going to face after release, but only a few are strong enough to lead themselves through the dehumanizing system and come out whole. How about you?"

"What do you mean?" Smoke's eyebrows draw together in confusion as he looks at Kenny.

"You're going to be 21 in a few months. Are you ready to lead your life, to become more than what the system expects from you?"

He shrugs. "I'm going to be all right."

"I know you're going to be alright my man," Kenny nods. "But I want you to be more than that. I want you to stand ready for whatever comes your way, strong enough to celebrate your successes in a responsible way, and more importantly, strong enough to lead your way back on the Straight-A path whenever you meet obstacles, or even failure."

"I already said, I'm going to write stories about the barrio, get my face on the cover of *Time* magazine." That testament from Smoke brings laughter from all.

"And I know you can do that if you work hard, but you've got to give a 100-percent effort—not the kind of halfway commitment I made when I signed on with the minor leagues for the Chicago White Sox and Kansas City Royals. Even if a man meets resistance, he's got to have the traits of leadership in him to stay the course, to keep following the path no matter what. Can you do that?"

Smoke nods his head.

"How about you, Trey? Can you keep walking the Straight-A path even if the first five video game developers choose not to offer you a job?"

"I'll just go on to the sixth developer," he shrugs. "Someone will give me a chance."

"Remember," Kenny warns the class, "no one has to give us anything. It's up to us to forge our own way. We use the Straight-A Guide to help us make decisions, but other people might not always act the way we want, the way we expect them to act. That's when our leadership skills come into play."

He double underlines the word on the board.

"If I can't find a job, I can always read another book on the subject, or I can write another letter to someone who is influential and might mentor me. I've got to lead in other words, take charge of my life, and when I do that, do you know what I develop?"

"Success?" Smoke ventures.

"Maybe," Kenny says, while writing the word 'character' on the board. "That all depends on how I define success. If it's getting a job, or getting my face on the cover of *Time* magazine that defines success for me, then I'm allowing the decisions of others to determine whether I succeed or not. But if I stay on the straight-A path no matter what, if my attitude is consistent with my aspirations, and all of my actions take me closer to the man I want to become, and I create a personal record that others can use to hold me accountable—then I create that awareness in myself and in others. I achieve. It's one thing to know the path, and it's another thing to walk the path. When I have all of that, I am a man of good character. That's what I want you to see."

With that he underlines *character*.

Success! The Straight-A Guide

✓ Integrity
✓ Leadership
✓ Character

The class responds well to Kenny. I wonder whether it's because they recognize his background as being similar to their own or because of his powerful presence. Regardless, the attention paid him is notable. What impresses the class most, I think, is his passion for the message. When he concludes and introduces Grande, the students reward Kenny with enthusiastic applause. Like Julius, Kenny is one of their own. Like Julius, Kenny gives hope.

Chapter Six

Osvaldo Richard Gonzalez
"Grande"

Grande hasn't been on an outing with our group before. He's in his late 20s and, as his nickname suggests, he's big: six-two and a solid 250. When Kenny calls his name, Grande stands, accidentally crushing my right foot. I clench my jaw to absorb the pain silently and join the students in clapping as he walks to the front of the class, leaving an open seat for Kenny.

"First of all I want to give a shout-out to whoever invited us to share our stories with you today, to you, officer," Grande exchanges a nod with the man with the gun. "And to our counselor from the prison, Ms. Martin, who authorized me to come along"

Counselor Martin sponsors our youth outreach group and meets with us every Wednesday morning to oversee our practice sessions. In that role she treats us kindly, encouraging our work to reconcile with society, and offering suggestions on how we can make our presentations more effective. All of us appreciate her effort. Without it we wouldn't have this opportunity to interact with others who might find value in our message. Counselor Martin smiles in acknowledgement, but continues to sit as a silent observer, allowing the rest of us to share our stories.

"Giving thanks is part of my new commitment to the Straight-A Guide," Grande begins, pointing to the word 'appreciate' on the blackboard behind him. "I may have more to appreciate than the others who are speaking with you today. They've all been walking this path for several years, but I'm kind of new to it and I'm glad to join them for the first time in coming out to share what I'm learning about making better decisions. It wasn't long ago that I was walking a different path—probably one that many of you have walked yourselves."

Grande pauses for a quick thought on how to proceed, then prefaces his remarks with a question.

"We're all talking today about making better decisions, or finding more direction in our lives. What I'd like to know is if there's anyone in the class who wanted to make better decisions before, but felt pressure from people he cared about that stopped him from making a change in his life. Did anyone ever feel that kind of competing force, wanting to do right but not knowing how to make a new start? I know I did."

The students stare at him, some fidgeting in their seats, not yet ready to make a commitment of speaking up or engaging with him. Grande waits. Finally—

"No one? Maybe if I explain a little about my life, someone will identify with what I'm trying to say."

He tells the group his name, Osvaldo Richard Gonzalez, but says his friends call him 'Rick' or 'Grande.' He's 29 and he's been in prison since he was 24, when he received a 15-year sentence for a drug conviction. His speech belies a nervous energy.

"Drugs aren't anything new in my life, nothing unusual. Ever since I was a small child I've been around drugs. I used to watch people close to me breaking down bricks of coke or bagging weed on the kitchen table when I was still riding tricycles."

A low chuckle breaks the class silence.

"You guys know what I'm talking about, right?" He laughs with them, breaking the ice and feeling more at ease. "Some of you know what it's like growing up in a crime family. I started selling drugs when I was 13. I was jumped in to a gang when I was 14. I've been carrying straps since I was 15, but this is my first time being busted. When I called home after my arrest, the only advice my dad had for me was not to snitch."

Grande tells the group that his mother would urge him to make something better of his life, but if selling drugs was okay for some members of his family then Grande didn't see any reason why he shouldn't do the same. The only positive influences of his young life came from his mother or those outside the family home, like a few high school teachers and football coaches.

"I played lineman on both offense and defense, even went on to play semi-pro ball and in the arena league for the California Predators. But my story isn't any different from what Julius or Kenny told you. My attitude toward a career in sports wasn't 100 percent, commitment wasn't all there. I kept on kicking it with the homies. Sometimes I thought about wanting to do right, to make a better life for myself, a fresh start. But I'd stay in, hustle the work, be down for whatever, always thinking I could make a change later. Anyone relate to that?"

A few of the students smirk, shift in their seats and mumble among themselves, but no one raises a hand.

"How about you?" Grande calls Smoke out. "I heard you say earlier that you've been in the system since you were 13, in and out. Didn't you ever lie in your cell at night, wondering what it would be like to sleep in a bed instead of on a metal rock? Didn't you feel as cold as the stone walls and steel doors that locked you inside, thinking that you'd like to make a fresh start?"

"Why's everyone singling me out?" Smoke complains with mock dismay, prompting more laughter from the class.

"Because we're all you, homie, just a few years down the line. No disrespect, I've got nothing but love for you," Grande pounds his heart. "I'm only trying to make sure you see what I was too much of a fool to see until I got trapped inside, with no way out until I finished a 15-year bid."

"Every time I been locked up I wanted to make a change," Smoke offers.

"Then I get out, you know what happens. The homies are all up on me, do this and that, putting the work in my hand. Before I know it, judge is either extending my probation or putting me up in the *pinta* again. It's a wrap in a couple of months. State won't have no more hold on me after I turn 21."

"Thing is," Grande advises, "even if you don't report to probation, without an attitude of 100 percent commitment to an aspiration, the homies are always going to be around to pull you back in. That message didn't get through to me when I was your age. If it had I could've done something better with my life than hustle dope. Some of the players I used to crash helmets against now play in the NFL. I sit in prison watching them on TV, mad at myself because I let pressure from the homies interfere with the commitment I should've made to football."

Grande describes for the group the thoughts that went through his head after arrest.

"DEA busted me in Iowa, more than a thousand miles away from my home turf in Southern Califas. You might think I'm crazy for saying this, Smoke, but in some ways me being busted wasn't much different from what you're about to go through in a few months, after you turn 21."

"You're right about that," Smoke says. "You are crazy if you think that my being cut loose from probation is anything like being busted." Smoke bumps fists with the student sitting to his left. "I'll be free, homie."

"It's not about being free, young homie, it's about *staying* free," Grande advises. "It's about being able to shake that attitude of the streets. It doesn't matter whether you're on the streets or locked inside cages. If you can't let go of the old attitude, you'll never resist the pressures from those around you. I didn't get that when I was first locked up, and before I knew it, I was all tangled up in new problems. You'll be 21, with a chance for a fresh start. I'd just turned 24 when I was locked up, but I also had a chance for a fresh start. That's what was the same for both of us, homie. Thing is, I didn't have the sense to take that chance for a fresh start. Pressures from the streets, same old attitude, sucked me in deeper. It took me a few years inside cages before I learned that it isn't a new environment, or even new conditions like graduating from school or finishing probation that bring a new start. A new start begins here and here," Grande points to his head and then his heart, "and it can only come with a new attitude."

"What do you mean 'pressures from the streets sucked you in deeper' once you were locked up? What went down?" Lump wants clarification from Grande.

Grande tells the class about his initial adjustment after his arrest. Not recognizing being locked up as an opportunity to redirect his life, Grande says that he started off his sentence with the same attitude he had in the streets. That attitude determined who he associated with inside. Being a long ways from home, he wanted to make a name for himself, to build a solid prison reputation.

"Before I knew it," Grande tells the class, "some fool who I considered my homie was snitching me off to the feds, bringing more heat down on me. If I would've started out with the right attitude, judge probably would've given me only 10 years. Instead I got 15 years. That only made me angrier, more determined to carve out my prison rep, doing what I had to do inside the fences. Check this out," Grande opens his shirt to reveal the Aztec warrior tattoos on his chest, with large, bold area code numbers of Southern California in the center. "These are only part of the tattoos I inked during my first two years in prison. They mark me for life, homie, a sign of the attitude I walked in with."

"What's wrong with the ink?" Trey asks. "Showing your colors, your pride in who you are."

"There's nothing wrong with ink or with showing pride," Grande says. "I am who I am and I'm always going to take pride in my cultural heritage, to represent. But let me tell you what the tattoos have done for me. Anytime I'm booked into a new prison, guards photograph all my ink. It identifies me as being gang affiliated. The guards don't harass me for it, but they send the photos into a police data base, letting law enforcement know who I am before I even say my name. The ink announces my old attitude, an attitude that wasn't leading me anywhere except into more problems."

"So do you regret getting the tattoos?" Smoke asks.

"I regret that it took me so long to put my life together, to understand that I couldn't cling to that same attitude from the streets if I didn't want to live with the consequences that came with it."

Grande pauses to reflect, then continues.

"That message didn't come to me until I was locked in the bucket with an older homie who was down 30 years on a life sentence. He had the prison reputation I was after, but he told me that he was living one drawn out death that he regretted. The homie told me that he hadn't touched a woman in longer than 20 years, that he would never know anything different from the cold steel bars of a prison. As I listened to him, I knew my attitude was going to bring on the same misery unless I made some changes. The *veterano* couldn't make those changes in his life anymore, but he schooled me on how I could change, and I listened. Now I'm trying to pass that message on to you."

"What kind of changes did you make?" Smoke's curiosity about how to make changes pleases me. I think Grande is reaching him, helping Smoke see that the potential for problems won't end with the conclusion of his probation.

Grande points back to the blackboard again. "Like the homies said before me, it all began with a change in my attitude. I started out this sentence with the attitude of building a prison reputation. That's what I was about in my early 20s. You live and learn. Those decisions resulted in my serving a longer sentence than I otherwise would have. They resulted in my starting out in higher security, spending too much time locked in SHU. When I changed my attitude, I changed everything else."

"How?" Lump asks.

"When the older homie who was serving life told me what I could expect if I didn't make a change, I realized that I didn't want any part of what he was describing. We spent a lot of time together, even when we got out of the bucket we kicked it on the yard. I respected him. He asked me to do something for him, and I was down for whatever. The homie blew me away with what he asked me to do."

"Yeah? What?"

Smoke senses that Grande is going to describe violence and he's ready to hear it.

"He told me he didn't like seeing so many of our people filling the jails and the prisons. The homie told me to do something better with my life so I wouldn't follow his footsteps into a life bid, and to educate myself so that I could make a positive difference in other people's lives. That's what I've been working towards ever since, and it's part of the reason I'm able to stand here today, sharing my story with you."

Not quite the answer Smoke was expecting.

Grande tries to explain the changes he made within the context of the Straight-A Guide that's still on the blackboard. While discussing attitude and aspirations, Grande elaborates on what it takes to build a prison reputation. He began his sentence aspiring for that respect, and he acted in ways that might one day elevate him to become the man on the yard, a shot caller.

"The actions that lead to respect from the other homies in prison," he explains, "only lead to more prison. After listening to some of the other homies I respected, I changed my aspirations."

Grande tells the group that the perceptions of other prisoners no longer govern his actions. "Thing is, I know who I am and I know *what* I am."

"What are you?" Smoke asks. "A prisoner?"

"I'm a man," Grande asserts. "And a man knows how to correct himself when he learns that he's been making bad decisions—decisions that can only lead to more prison time or death. That's what I picked up from the *veteranos*. Instead of living with an attitude from the streets, I now make all my decisions with the attitude of overcoming the challenges I expect to face when I get out." Grande has the entire class's attention as he hammers home his message.

"How're you going to know what's waiting for you then?" Jay asks. "You still got eight years to go. That's like forever."

"It is what it is. Whenever they let me out, I know that I'm going to have to meet a probation officer to serve three years of supervised release. I know that I'm going to have to explain myself to people who might consider me for a job. When I make decisions now, they don't come with the attitude and aspiration of making a name for myself in prison. My attitude is all about preparing so that once they let me out, I never have to look at the world from the inside of a cage again. I've got aspirations of working with young people, of influencing them in ways that will help them resist pressures from the streets that pull so many of our people into jails and prisons."

"That's all cool," Smoke says. "You and your homies wanting to make big changes in the world and all that. But why you doing that now, when you're locked in the *pinta*? Why didn't you make those changes before you were locked up?"

"It's right there on the board, homie. I might not have understood it before, but back then I didn't want to change. My attitude was all about the streets, about being down." Grande shakes his head. "I didn't see it then, wasn't thinking about where my decisions were leading me."

"You're telling me you were hustling dope, gang banging, but you never thought about doing time? That don't make sense."

"It's not that I didn't think about serving time," Grande corrects him. "I didn't care about serving time because I wasn't thinking about something better. It wasn't until I started serving time and listening to the people I respected telling me about what it's like to live without ever expecting to hold a woman again, without ever being a father or someone more than a prisoner, that I opened my eyes. Now I see. Now I want something more out of life, not only for me but for all my people, including you."

Grande describes the actions he has begun to take. He is now a college student, working through four classes a semester that will lead to his college degree. He's participating in the youth outreach program. He's developing his writing and communication skills, including drawing, in order to prepare for his aspiration of a career teaching others.

"You might see me as a prisoner, dressed in a khaki uniform, but the steps I'm taking every day will lead me somewhere else. Someday I'll stand in front of an audience of people, lots of people, and I'll motivate them with a message about how changing attitudes leads to higher aspirations. I'll tell them that actions can change the direction of their lives. I'll describe how following the Straight-A Guide led me to hold myself accountable, how it opens my awareness. I celebrate every achievement, and I appreciate every source of encouragement, including from all of you."

Conclusion

The class applauds after Grande's presentation and the three of us stand in front of the students to answer their questions. Despite the clouds of cynicism and pessimism we felt earlier, the students now encourage us with their animated interactions. Instead of asking about the violence, the gangs, and the hustles of prison life, their questions reflect an interest in changing, in opening opportunities, in embracing the Straight-A Guide.

Individual states spend more than $100,000 per year to lock up each juvenile offender, but high recidivism rates show that warehousing human beings is not the solution for America's crime problem.

Rather than extinguishing hope for at-risk adolescents and young offenders, society should recognize that it has a vested interest in providing them with education and opportunities.

The other prisoners with whom I work recognize that we have responsibilities. We did not make good decisions as young men, and the consequences we faced came with heavy prices. In my case, that price has been a quarter century in prison. Others may not serve as long as me, but we all made bad choices and we bear the scars that followed.

In describing our commitment to emerge as law-abiding citizens, we hope to provide our audience with an insightful message that none of us received as young men: the Straight-A Guide is the path to success.

Make a 100-percent commitment to keep a positive *attitude*; *aspire* to make better decisions; take incremental *actions* that lead to those aspirations; embrace *accountability*; create *awareness*; celebrate *achievements* along the way; and express *appreciation* for every blessing that comes.

MICHAEL G. SANTOS FOUNDATION

Outreach Programs for At-Risk Youth and Successful Offender Reentry

The Michael G. Santos Foundation (MGSF) provides programs and resources to prepare at-risk youth and adult offenders for law-abiding, fulfilling, contributing lives. Through its work, MGSF strives to strengthen the fabric of society by offering strategies every individual can use to triumph over adversity and reach their highest potential in areas that include:

- Education
- Employment
- Fitness
- Relationships
- Community leadership

Program materials include the following books by Michael G. Santos:

- *Prison! My 8,344th Day*
- *Success! The Straight-A Guide*
- *Earning Freedom: My Triumph Over a 45-Year Prison Term*

Please visit our Web site for more information about the resources and services available through the Michael G. Santos Foundation.

www.MichaelSantos.org

501 (C)(3) Tax Exempt #: 27-1904346

Other Books by Michael G. Santos

Inside: Life Behind Bars in America (St. Martin's Press)

Michael Santos shows readers what it's like to live in America's jails and prisons. Using the voice of the penitentiary, he graphically describes a system infested with gangs, drugs, beatings, shanks, and extortion. From meth-crazed prisoners raping the weak, to female guards who prostitute themselves with the help of gang leaders, and murders in protective custody, Santos brings readers as close as they'll ever want to come to confinement.

About Prison (Wadsworth Publishing)

In this unique and extraordinary text, Michael G. Santos helps others learn about the abnormal way of life behind the walls and fences of prisons. To provide readers with a more complete and realistic picture of the growing subculture that exists in prison, Santos provides both his own experiences and observations of living as a prisoner, as well as dialogues, vignettes, and profiles of other prisoners and workers within the prison environment.

Profiles From Prison (Praeger Publishing,)

Santos offers the gripping stories of men serving a variety of terms, providing commentary and analysis as he guides readers through the prison experience. Sections of the book are based on length of imprisonment. Some describe the actions that lead to their confinement, or detail the complexities of living in all-male communities. Others reveal the ways they cope with their terms, or the expectations for life after prison.

Prison! My 8,344th Day (APS Publishing)

In this short, easy to read book, Michael Santos provides an inside look at his typical day. *Prison*! is the astounding story of how one man, after serving 23 years in institutions that are known for extinguishing all hope, will soon leave prison filled with hope and dignity intact. Readers of all ages can learn from Mr. Santos' description of discipline, commitment, and values-based, goal-centered decisions.